*Acclaim for Rick Bragg's*

# Ava's Man

"A book that works on many levels . . . perhaps above all as just grand storytelling."          —*The Boston Globe*

"The book preserves the dignity of a much-maligned region, but *Ava's Man* succeeds as art, unattached to place."          —*The New York Times*

"Rick Bragg has once more gone to the well of his family's history and drawn readers a story that goes down like a long drink of sweet spring water—with a little taste of whiskey on the side."
          —*Minneapolis Star Tribune*

"Celebrates the working people of the Deep South with the passion of a novelist and the precision of a memoirist."          —*The Atlanta Journal-Constitution*

"Rich in the raw materials of character and local color, enhanced by language marked with extravagance and economy—and the born storyteller's gift for knowing when to be lavish with words and when to be lean."
          —*St. Louis Post-Dispatch*

*Rick Bragg*

# Ava's Man

Rick Bragg is the bestselling author of *All Over but the Shoutin'* and *Somebody Told Me*. A national correspondent for *The New York Times*, he was awarded the Pulitzer Prize for feature writing in 1996. He lives in New Orleans.

# Ava's Man

# Ava's Man

## Rick Bragg

Vintage Books
A Division of Random House, Inc.
New York

FIRST VINTAGE BOOKS EDITION, SEPTEMBER 2002

The Library of Congress has cataloged the Knopf edition as follows:
Bragg, Rick.
Ava's man / Rick Bragg.
p. cm.
ISBN 0-375-41062-7
1. Bundrum, Charlie.  2. Working class whites—Southern States—
Biography.  3. Depressions—1929—Southern States.  4. Southern States—
Social life and customs—20th century.  5. Southern States—Biography.
I. Title.
CT275.B78516  B73  2001b
975'.042'092—dc21
[B]  2001032677

**Vintage ISBN: 0-375-72444-3**

*Book design by Iris Weinstein*

www.vintagebooks.com

Printed in the United States of America
10  9  8  7  6  5  4  3  2  1

*To Ava and Charlie*
   *and the children*

*James, William, Edna, Juanita, Margaret, Jo,*
   *Sue, and Little Emma Mae*

*And the grandchildren,*
*And the great-grandchildren,*
*And the ones who come after*

# Contents

# Ava's Man

*On the Big Rock Candy Mountain*
*The police have wooden legs*
*The bulldogs all have rubber teeth*
*And the hens lay soft-boiled eggs*
*The trees let down their rich, ripe fruit*
*And you sleep on silky hay*
*And the wind don't blow and there ain't no snow*
*Forever and a day*
—A SONG FROM THE GREAT DEPRESSION

# On a bluebird day

She was old all my life. Even when I was sitting in the red dirt, fascinated with my own toes, Ava's face had a line in it for every hot mile she ever walked, for every fit she ever threw. Her hair was long and black as crows, streaked with white, and her eyes, behind the ancient, yellowed glass of her round spectacles, were pale, pale blue, almost silver. The blind have eyes like that, that color, but Ava could see fine, Ava could see forever. She could tell your fortune by gazing into the dregs of your coffee cup, and swore that if the bottoms of your feet itched, you would walk on strange ground. She could be gentle as a baby bird and sweet as divinity candy, but if her prescription was off, or if she just got mad, she would sit bolt upright in bed at three o'clock in the morning and dog-cuss anyone who came to mind, including the dead. Some days she would doze in her rocker and speak softly to people that I could not find, even by looking under the porch. Now I know I was just listening to her dreams.

In her time she buried two daughters, one just a baby, one full-grown, and when she passed eighty my aunts just stopped telling her when people she loved had died. A kindness, I suppose. Near the end of her life, as her mind began to wobble, she would recall how pretty my ex-wife looked at Christmas dinner eighteen years ago, yet not remember yesterday. But when I think of her now I think of a woman still strong and hard in her late sixties, a woman with a banjo propped against the foot of her bed, ten thousand hairpins in the pocket of her dress and more personalities than the state hospital in Tuscaloosa. I think about how the sudden summer thunderstorms would rattle the window glass and make cups jump off their saucers, and how, unimpressed, the old woman would just take a dip of snuff and mumble, "Ol' devil's beatin' his wife."

Because she was old, and could be trusted with babies and half-wits, it was her job to watch over me when my momma, her sixth child, went to work. She would look down on me from her rocker, talking to me and, as she grew older, herself. In time I could even gauge that old woman's mood by the pace of her chair's squeaking runners on the bare pine planks—slow when her mind was restful, quick when she was mad, and fast, racehorse fast, when she was remembering. The sheer power of it would send those runners to squeaking fierce and hot, back and forth, and to this day I still wonder why the whole damn thing didn't blaze up from the friction of it, and burn the house down.

She had been widowed young and never remarried, and as a child I just assumed she had always been that way, an old woman alone. There was a man once, a peddler for the Saxon Candy Company who seemed to have a lot more on his mind than salt-water taffy. But if that little ol' man was a suitor, he was pitiful at it, and he did not give up so much as just timidly fade away. That did not stop her grandchildren from kidding her about him, from asking if she was going to run off with him someday in his panel truck full of pecan logs.

"Grandma," we would ask, in a joke that spanned twenty years, "you goin' to get you a man?"

Most times she just sniffed and ignored us, but sometimes she would slap her heavy black shoes down hard on the porch, applying the brakes, and the rocker's runners would freeze in mid-squeak. We fled, usually, because she was prone to strike out, quick as a rattler, and knock us upside the head when she was displeased. But instead of hollering or swinging at us, she would just start to grin, as if something that had gone cold in her memory had begun to glow for just a second or two in time. It was probably just her medicine again, but it is better to believe it was a speck of heat from something that had once crackled and roared along the banks of the Coosa River back when it was wild, in the days before the power company dams turned it into a big brown faucet that could be switched on and off at will.

"No, hon," she would say, "I ain't goin' to get me no man." And then she would start to rock again, with satisfaction.

"I had me one."

\* \* \*

His name was Charlie Bundrum and he was probably the only man on earth who could love that woman and not perish in the flame.

He was a tall, bone-thin man who worked with nails in his teeth and a roofing hatchet in a fist as hard as Augusta brick, who ran a trot-line across the Coosa baited with chicken guts and caught washtubs full of catfish, who cooked good white whiskey in the pines, drank his own product and sang, laughed and buck-danced, under the stars. He was a man whose tender heart was stitched together with steel wire, who stood beaten and numb over a baby's grave in Georgia, then took a simple-minded man into his home to protect him from scoundrels who liked to beat him for fun. He was a man who inspired backwoods legend and the kind of loyalty that still makes old men dip their heads respectfully when they say his name, but who was bad to drink too much, miss his turn into the driveway and run over his own mailbox.

He was a man who did the things more civilized men dream they could, who beat one man half to death for throwing a live snake at his son, who shot a large woman with a .410 shotgun when she tried to cut him with a butcher knife, who beat the hell out of two worrisome Georgia highway patrolmen and threw them headfirst out the front door of a beer joint called the Maple on the Hill. He was a man who led deputies on long, hapless chases across high, lonesome ridges and through brier-choked bogs, whose hands were so quick he snatched squirrels from trees, who hunted without regard to seasons or quotas, because how could a game warden in Montgomery or Atlanta know if his babies were hungry?

He was just a man, I guess, whose wings never quite fit him right, who built dozens of pretty houses for Depression-era wages and never managed to build one for the people he loved the most, who could not read but always asked Ava to read him the newspaper so he would not be ignorant, who held iron bars and babies in his massive hands and called my momma "Pooh Boy," which makes me smile.

He died in the spring of 1958, one year before I was born.

I have never forgiven him for that.

\* \* \*

For most of my life he was no more real, no more complete, than a paper doll. I learned, scrap by scrap, that he was a carpenter, roofer, whiskey maker, sawmill hand, well digger, hunter, poacher and river man, born at the turn of the century in a part of the country that is either Alabama or Georgia, depending on how lost you are, or if you even care. But I knew almost nothing else about him growing up, because no one in my momma's family talked much about him. As years and even decades slipped by, I began to wonder if I would uncover anything at all about my grandfather, or if he would just remain a man of secrets I would never know.

It could not be, I knew, that his children were ashamed of him—the flashes of his life they had let slip, from time to time, were bright, quick and warm, a sliver of light under a closed door. But in a family rich in storytellers, they were stingy with him, just him. It always left me with the same feeling I used to get when we would drive past the giant Merita bread factory in Birmingham. The smell of baking bread, mouthwatering, would fill the car for just a few seconds, then vanish as we sped on, leaving me daydreaming about sandwiches.

I asked my momma, two Christmases ago, why I had heard so little about him from her and her sisters. She told me that it was just a matter of time.

Only in the past few years, as his oldest son passed seventy, as his children marked the forty-second anniversary of their father's death, was there enough space between then and now to talk about him, to really remember. In the past, talking about his life always led to thinking of his death, to a feeling like running your fingers through saw briers—and what good is that?

"After Daddy died," my momma told me, "it was like there was nothin'."

I remember the night, an icy night in December, I asked three of Charlie Bundrum's daughters to tell me about his funeral. I sat in embarrassment as my aunts, all in their sixties, just stared hard at the floor. Juanita, tough as whalebone and hell, began to softly cry, and Jo, who has survived Uncle John and ulcers, wiped at her eyes. My mother, Margaret, got up and left the room. For coffee, she said.

What kind of man was this, I wondered, who is so beloved, so missed, that the mere mention of his death would make them cry forty-two years after he was preached into the sky?

A man like that, I thought to myself, probably deserves a book.

I had a grandfather, another, who really did get drunk, hitch his wagon and drive through the mill village of my hometown shouting dirty limericks to church ladies and Jehovah Witnesses until the town sheriff hauled him away, in chains. But my daddy's daddy, Bobby Bragg, though entertaining as hell, had never seemed to claim us. He was not cruel, merely indifferent, and between rants and incarcerations he would do his best not to step on us, very much, as we played on his porch.

So, since I never really had a grandfather, I decided to make me one. I asked my mother's people to tell me all the stories they could remember from Charlie Bundrum's life and times. With their help, I built him up from dirt level, using half-forgotten sayings, half-remembered stories and a few yellowed, brittle, black-and-white photographs that, under the watch of my kin, I handled like diamonds.

Two, in particular, tell his story. In one, he is dressed in his Sunday-go-to-meetin' clothes, not his overalls, but his big wrists and scarred, tar-stained, gnarled hands tell on him. The face staring out from under a misshapen straw slouch hat looks tense and hard-edged, as if it can't wait for this foolishness to be over, and the eyes bore into you, challenge you. It is a studio photo, taken on Noble Street in Anniston, Alabama, in front of a painted-on palm.

A poor man, posing.

"That ain't Daddy," my aunt Jo said.

The one I love to look at, the one I have on my living room wall, is more honest. He is wearing ragged overalls, faded to gray, the legs specked with what seems to be fish blood, and he is prison-camp thin. In one big hand, strong fingers hooked through its gills, is a catfish three feet long, its head as broad as a bull calf.

A poor man, winning.

"I remember when we were little and we would wait for him to come in from the job," said my aunt Gracie Juanita, thinking back to one night—or maybe many, many nights—when she was a child. "We would be playin', and Momma would already have supper done. And then it would come up a cloud, and I was so scared.

"Then Daddy would come in the door, and it was like, well, like the sky had cleared. And we weren't afraid of nothin', because he wasn't afraid of nothin'." Then she just looked at me, hard, in that way that old women look at you when they tell you something private, something almost secret, and fear you will not feel it as strong as they do—or, worse, not believe.

"Ricky," said my momma from across the room, "she's tellin' God's sanction. It was like the sky cleared."

Maybe all men like that deserve a book.

The challenge in telling Charlie Bundrum's story, I soon found out, was how to do it without being disowned, and probably slapped, by one of my sainted aunts. If I ever let his wings drag in the dust, his surviving daughters would do more than forget my birthday.

But he is so much more precious smelling of hot cornbread and whiskey than milk and honey. His story is more important knowing how the moonshine made him sing instead of cuss, knowing how he did fight, with bared teeth and blood in his eye, the people who insulted him or brought trouble to his door. He is more beloved because he truly did ride into their yard late in the evenings, passed out cold on the back of his saddle horse, Bob, who would gently shrug him to the grass before trotting into his stall.

The one thing I am dead sure of is that his ghost, conjured in a hundred stories, would have haunted me forever if I had whitewashed him. He was, I am told, usually a quiet man, not given to foolishness, who would ride the river in his homemade boats for hours, silent, or sit with a baby in the crook of his arm on the front porch, humming a railroad song. But when the spirit—or the likker—moved him, he was one of the finest storytellers who ever lived in our part of the country, a spinner of beautiful campfire stories and notorious tall tales, a man who didn't need a gun to kill you because he was capable of talking you to death. A man like that, surely, would want a legacy with pepper on it.

But as it turned out, they need not have worried what people would say about him. I spoke to distant cousins and tiny, frail great-aunts, to old men with no reason to lie and some, my aunts warned me, who lied with every quavering breath. They all said the same thing—that he was a damn rascal, all right, but he was their damn rascal, and they ought to stick a statue of him up smack-dab in the middle of the square in Jacksonville, Alabama, next to the Confederate soldier.

"He was a hero," said Travis Bundrum, his great-nephew, a sad-eyed, silver-haired man who fished the brown Coosa with him in a boat made from two car hoods welded together. His great-uncle Charlie—most people here pronounce it "Chollie"—saved his life on a dark night on that river fifty years ago, one more piece of the legend that people tell over macaroni and cheese and pork chops at the family reunions.

"He ought to have a monument," Travis says, "because there ain't no more like him. All his kind are gone."

In a time when a nation drowning in its poor never so resented them, in the lingering pain of Reconstruction, in the Great Depression and in the recovery that never quite reached all the way to my people, Charlie Bundrum took giant steps in run-down boots. He grew up in a hateful poverty, fought it all his life and died with nothing except a family that worshiped him and a name that gleams like new money. When he died, mourners packed Tredegar Congregational Holiness Church. Men in overalls and oil-stained jumpers and women with hands stung red from picking okra sat by men in dry-cleaned suits and women in dresses bought on Peachtree Street, and even the preacher cried.

*  *  *

Looking back on it, I do not think I have ever had so much fun as I have had in learning and sharing the stories of a man that history would otherwise have ignored, as it would have ignored my mother and people like her, the working people of the Deep South. In her story, a book that people just call *Shoutin',* I introduced Charlie and Ava and their children, but I was in too much of a rush, people told me. I left out the good part.

At book signings, in letters, in encounters on the street, people asked me where I believed my own momma's heart and backbone came from, where she inherited the strength and character to sacrifice herself in those endless cotton fields, to raise three boys alone. And why did that work—with the indignities of welfare and the disdain of the better-off—not burn away her sense of humor, the part of her that shines?

But before I could answer, they answered for me. They said I short-shrifted them in the first book, especially about Charlie, about Ava, about their children. That, they say, is the root of it, the answer. That, people lectured me on the phone and harangued me in airports, is the beginning.

I wrote this story for a lot of reasons, but for that above all others—to give one more glimpse into a vanishing culture for the people who found themselves inside such stories, the people who shook my hand and said, "Son, you stole my story."

Some of them would admit, shamefully, that they battled with the past all their lives and never quite knew whether to be proud of their people or ashamed. Some even pretended that there was no past, that they had no history before sorority rush, or induction into the Mason lodge. For them, the past was a door they locked themselves—but in the closet late at night they could always hear those rattling bones.

But I am proud of Charlie Bundrum. I want my grandfather to walk out of the past—with Ava, God rest her soul, beside him. If what I have heard about Charlie and Ava is true, he would not have minded having just a little bit of a head start on her, so he could have some fun before she got there.

As for me, I got what I came for.

Charlie Bundrum, though I never even saw his face, would have wanted us. He would have held us high in one of those legendary hands, like a new bulldog puppy, and laughed out loud. He would have watched over us, slipping us Indian head pennies and Mercury dimes. And every Friday, when my momma went into town to cash her check, he would have fed nickels into the mechanized bucking horse outside the A&P, to see us ride.

I am not sure of that because it's what I want, because it's the way a boy would have built himself a grandfather. But the actual man, a flawed and sometimes boozy man, would have done it all, if he had lived. I am sure of this because that actual man lived just long enough to reach for one of us, a boy older than me, and prove it.

* * *

In the fall of 1997, an Alabama newspaper sent a reporter to interview my mother. I sat in her living room on the chert hill in northeastern Alabama and shook my head as she deftly deflected the reporter's questions about her sacrifices, about her hard life, and laughed when she said she was just walking around the house in her old age, trying not to fall off the pedestal that I had put her on.

Then the reporter, a nice lady from Birmingham, asked her to recall the best day of her life. It was a splendid question. I wrote one whole book about her, and forgot to ask it.

I thought my momma, who had lived her life in borrowed houses, might say that it was the day I handed her the keys to her own home—partial payment of a debt I will never really repay. Or I thought she would say it was the day that *Shoutin'*, a book that honored her, was printed, and I handed her a copy with her face on the cover.

I should have known better. Books and houses. Paper and wood.

"I believe," she said, "it was the birth of my first son, Sam."

It was the eleventh of September 1956, and Daddy was absent, which was a cause for concern but not alarm. He would show up sooner or later, in weeks or months, as soon as he had drank Korea away, as soon as the faces of dead men had slipped once more beneath the calm brown surface of bootleg whiskey.

When Daddy left he took the rent with him, so she had nowhere else to take the baby except home. Charlie and Ava lived in a rented house on Alabama 21, in the woods behind Wright's store, and she took him there. What is it people say about home? It is where you go when no one else wants you.

My grandfather took the baby in his hands, engulfing him, and grinned.

"By God, Margaret," he said, "you've got Samson here." And he held him for hours.

No one slept much that night. The next day my grandfather, grumbling but good-natured, said it was too damn noisy to rest. It wasn't that the baby had cried. The baby had not cried at all.

"Margaret," he said, "you kept us up all night, a'talkin' to that boy."

My momma stopped then, done, as if the rest of the story, the best part, was hers alone. Finally the reporter asked her: "Well, what were you saying?"

"I just kept whisperin'," she said, "over and over, 'You're mine. You're mine.'

"I never did have anything," she said, which is as close as I have ever heard her come to feeling sorry, even a little, for herself. It was just that she wanted her visitor to understand.

"I didn't even have a doll. But he was mine. He belonged to me."

I understood. I had heard her tell stories of the poverty she and her brothers and sisters had been born to, heard them all recount hard times with that benign nonchalance of their generation, like the poverty was some mean dog that had long since died from old age. Even with a daddy who worked hard, luxury was a piece of hard penny candy, plucked from a tiny brown-paper sack. It melted, in minutes.

But now here was this amazing, tiny thing, and she would have him, with luck, all of her life. And as long as her own father lived, the boy would be protected as she had always been protected. Only the generation had changed, not his character. The sky would still clear.

They got so much more than that. Charlie Bundrum, in the last year of his life, seemed to focus all his love, all his attention, on Sam. He would rest in the yard with one long, skinny leg crossed over the other, and for hours he would talk to the baby, sing to him, just look at him. He drilled a hole in a silver dime and put it on string, then slipped it over the boy's head. He carried him around on his hip or in the crook of his arm, and recited senseless rhymes . . .

> *Ain't goin' to town*
> *Ain't goin' to city*
> *Goin' on down*
> *To Diddy-Wah-Diddy*

. . . until the baby would laugh.

He would buy soft candy, in the shape of a peanut, and hide it in the bib pocket of his overalls. Sam learned, over time, that it was there, and would go prowling through the pocket with such dead-serious intent that my grandfather would just sit and laugh.

At night, as my grandfather slept, the boy would toddle over to the coal bin and pick up a piece of coal, then toddle back across the room and drop the lump in one of my grandfather's work boots. He would repeat the process, over and over, as my momma and grandmother sat and smiled, until he had filled both boots full of coal. Sam was single-minded, even then, and when he was done he would look proudly at my momma and gurgle something, as if to say, "See what a fine boy you have?" Then she would scoop him up and scrub his hands clean, to get rid of the evidence.

In the morning my grandfather would awaken, and without even glancing at the boy he would reach down, pick up his sooty boots and dump the coal back into the bin, wearily shaking his head, mumbling, "Now how do you reckon that got in there? Must be fairies."

Sometimes, in the mornings, the still-young man would hold his side, from sharp pains deep, deep inside him, but would go off to work anyway, if he had a house to roof that day. If he didn't have work, he scooped up the boy and walked outside, a worn-down man and a brand-new one, killing time.

"Daddy," Momma told me, a lifetime later, "was a fool over Sam."

Part of the story I had heard before, about the day my daddy came for them, how Charlie Bundrum told him to git or take a whippin', then told my momma she was grown and could make up her own mind, but if she left, she could not take Sam. She did not return to my daddy until her father died, when Sam was not yet three years old. Life was hard after that, for a real long time.

"I've always figured that if Daddy had lived he would have killed your daddy, for the way he treated us," she told me, softly, almost in a whisper. It was not just something to say. It was something that would have happened.

People still say what a shame it was that he died so young, at fifty-one, but I cannot say he died too soon. He lived long enough to see most of his children grown. He lasted, with his liver and heart ravaged by whiskey and hard living, till my brother Sam came into this world, and then he hung on, to save my mother and big brother from the sadness beyond his door, for as long as he could.

Sam, being so small, remembers almost none of it, none of it except the candy in the bib pocket of the overalls. That he recalls dim and dreamy, and vaguely sweet. He does not remember getting that dime on the string. He just knows he has always had it.

\* \* \*

One fall day, a lifetime later, we were fishing at a lake bracketed by the Roy Webb Road and Carpenter's Lane, casting rubber worms into the dense duck weed, not saying much, just living. All my life Sam has outfished me, and I've come to expect his amused, pitying look as I reel in my spinner bait with a big dollop of algae on the hook and nothing else. I know I should not care about that, but I do, because he is my big brother and forever will be, even when we sit one day wheezing and befuddled in the county home.

But that day, the world was upside down. I cast into a clear spot in the weed and caught a nice little bass, and then another, and another. I caught six. He did not catch any.

We finally decided to pick up the tackle and go on home, and it was hard for me, a grown man, not to just prance around and around him in a circle.

Sam just slipped the rods into the back of the Ford Bronco and, without even looking at me, dismissed the whole afternoon with a grunt. "Ricky," he said, "I was fishin' for the big fish."

Then he stared up at a perfect blue sky, a sky without a cloud.

"And everybody knows," he said, "the big fish won't bite on a bluebird day."

I just looked at him, because I did not have a rock to throw. On the one day I outfish him, he is spouting poetry.

Yet I could not help but wonder where that phrase, that lovely phrase, came from. Who still talks like that, I wondered, in a modern-day South that has become so homogenized, so bland, that middle school children in Atlanta make fun of people who sound Southern? I found out it was just something my grandfather and men like him used to say, something passed down to him, to us, like a silver pocket watch.

A man like Charlie Bundrum doesn't leave much else, not title or property, not even letters in the attic. There's just stories, all told second- and thirdhand, as long as somebody remembers. The thing to do, if you can, is write them down on new paper.

# The beatin' of Blackie Lee

*The foothills of the Appalachians*

THE 1930S

Ava met him at a box-lunch auction outside Gadsden, Alabama, when she was barely fifteen, when a skinny boy in freshly washed overalls stepped from the crowd of bidders, pointed to her and said, "I got one dollar, by God." In the evening they danced in the grass to a fiddler and banjo picker, and Ava told all the other girls she was going to marry that boy someday, and she did. But to remind him that he was still hers, after the cotton rows aged her and the babies came, she had to whip a painted woman named Blackie Lee.

Maybe it isn't quite right to say that she whipped her. To whip somebody, down here, means there was an altercation between two people, and somebody, the one still standing, won. This wasn't that. This was a beatin', and it is not a moment that glimmers in family history. But of all the stories I was told of their lives together, this one proves how Ava loved him, and hated him, and which emotion won out in the end.

Charlie Bundrum was what women here used to call a purty man, a man with thick, sandy hair and blue eyes that looked like something you would see on a rich woman's bracelet. His face was as thin and spare as the rest of him, and he had a high-toned, chin-in-the-air presence like he had money, but he never did. His head had never quite caught up with his ears, which were still too big for most human beings, but the women of his time were not particular as to ears, I suppose.

He was also a man who was not averse to stopping off at the bootlegger's now and again, and that was where he encountered a traveling woman with crimson lipstick and silk stockings named Blackie Lee. People called her Blackie because of her coal-black hair, and when she told my granddaddy that she surely was parched and tired and sure would 'preciate a place to wash her clothes and rest a spell before she moved on down the road, he told her she was welcome at his house.

They were living in north Georgia at that time, outside Rome. Ava and the five children—there was only James, William, Edna, Juanita and Margaret then—were a few miles away, working in Newt Morrison's cotton field. Charlie always took in strays—dogs, men and women, who needed a place—but Blackie was a city woman and pretty, too, which set the stage for mayhem.

It all might have gone unnoticed. Blackie Lee might've washed her clothes, set a spell and then just moved along, if that was all that she was after. But we'll never know. We'll never know because she had the misfortune to hang her stockings on Ava Bundrum's clothesline in front of God and everybody.

Miles away from there, Ava was hunched over in the cotton field, dragging a heavy sack, her fingers and thumbs on fire from the needle-sharp stickers on the cotton bolls. Newt Morrison's daughter, Sis, came up alongside of her in the field, one row over, and lit the fuse.

"Ava," said Sis, who had driven past Ava and Charlie's house earlier that day, "did you get you some silk stockings?"

Ava said no she had not, what foolishness, and just picked on.

"Well," Sis said, "is your sister Grace visitin' you?"

No, Ava said, if Grace had come to visit, she would have written or sent word.

"Well," said Sis, "I drove past y'all's place and seen some silk stockings on the line, and I thought they must have been Grace's, 'cause she's the only one I could think of that would have silk stockings."

Ava said well, maybe it was Grace, and picked on. Grace had wed a rich man and had silk stockings and a good car and may have come by, just on a whim. That must be it. Had to be.

Edna, then only a little girl, said her momma just kept her back bowed and her face down for a few more rows, then jerked bolt upright as if she had been stung by a bee, snatched the cotton sack from her neck and flung it, heavy as it was, across two rows.

Then she just started walking, and the children, puzzled, hurried after her. Even as an old woman Ava could walk most people plumb into the ground, and as a young woman she just lowered her head and swung her arms and kicked up dust as she powered down the dirt road to home.

When she swung into the yard, sometime later, it was almost dark and Blackie Lee was on the porch, cooling herself. Ava stopped and drew a breath and just looked at her for a moment, measuring her for her coffin. Then she stomped over to the woodpile and picked up the ax.

About that time it must have dawned on Blackie Lee who this young woman was, who these big-eyed children were, and she ran inside, put the latch down on the door and began to speak to Jesus.

Ava just stood there, breathing hard, her long hair half in and half out of her dew rag, and announced that the woman could either open the door and take her beatin' or take her beatin' after Ava hacked down her own door. And "you might not want me to walk in thar, with a' ax in my hand." Blackie Lee, hysterical, unlatched the door and stepped back, and Ava, as she promised, dropped the ax and stepped inside.

She might not have beat the woman quite so bad if it had not been for the dishpan. It had dirty water in it, from that woman's clothes. No one, no one, washed their clothes in Ava's dishpan.

Edna stood at the door, peeking.

Listen to her:

"Momma beat her all through the house. She beat her out onto the porch, beat her out into the yard and beat her down to the road, beat her so hard that her hands swelled up so big she couldn't fit 'em in her apron pocket. Then she grabbed aholt of her with one hand and used the other hand to flag down a car that was comin', and she jerked open that car door and flung that woman in and told the man drivin' that car to get her 'on outta here.' And that man said, 'Yes, ma'am,' and drove off with Blackie Lee."

Charlie was at work when this happened, which was very fortunate, so fortunate that even now his children swear there was God's hand in it. Even with temptation at his house, he went off to work and made a living, and it saved him, it saved everything. A weak man would have just laid out that day, and if he had been home Ava would have killed him dead as Julius Caesar.

Ava and the five children went back to Newt Morrison's to spend the night. Newt was distant kin and Ava knew she was welcome there. But first she walked inside her house and threw that dishpan out into the yard as far as she could.

That night, Charlie showed up to take them home. And Ava lit into him so hard and so fast that Charlie lost one of his shoes in the melee and had to fight from an uneven platform, which is bad when you have what seems to be a badger crawling and spittin' around your head. They fought, Edna said, all the way down the hall, crashing hard into the wall, making a hellish racket and scaring everybody in there to death. Children screamed and dogs barked and Charlie just kept on hollerin' over and over, "Dammit, Ava. Quit." Finally they crashed onto a bed, and into the room walked the old man, Newt, barefoot, one of his overall galluses on and one off. Newt thought that it was Charlie who was beating his wife to death, instead of the other way around, and all he knew was that this boy, Charlie, kin or not, had invaded his home, rattled the walls and frightened his family.

Newt, stooped and gray and gnarly, was much too old to fist-fight a man in his own house. So he reached into his overalls pocket, fished out his pocketknife and flicked out a blade long enough to cut watermelon.

Ava took one look at that knife and flung her body across her husband, to shield him. Then she looked up at Newt, and when she spoke there were spiders and broken glass in her voice.

"Don't you touch him," she hissed.

\* \* \*

Everybody has a moment like it. If they never did, they never did love nobody, truly. People who have lived a long, long time say it, so it must be so.

\* \* \*

They never spoke about it. They never had another moment like it again. They fought—my Lord, did they fight—for thirty years, until the children were mostly grown and gone. But they stuck. You go through as much as they did, you stick. I have seen old people do it out of spite, as if growing old together was some sweet revenge. Charlie and Ava did not get to grow old together. What they got was life condensed, something richer and sweeter and—yes—more bitter and violent, life with the dull moments just boiled or scorched away.

She never bowed to him, and he never made her, and they lived that way, in the time they had.

Every now and then, they would jab a little. She would stand over her new dishpan and recite a little poem as she gently rinsed her iron skillet and biscuit pans:

> *Single life is a happy life*
> *Single life is a pleasure*
> *I am single and no man's wife*
> *And no man can control me*

He would pretend not to hear. And bide his time, to get even.

"Daddy," Margaret would ask him when she was still a little girl, "how come you haven't bought us a radio?"

Charlie would just shake his head.

"Hon, we don't need no radio," he would say, and then he would point one of his long, bony fingers at Ava. "I already got a walkie-talkie."

And on and on it went, them pretending, maybe out of pride, that they did not love each other, and need each other, as much as they did.

As time dragged on they would break out the banjo—Charlie was hell-hot on a banjo—and the guitar, which Ava played a lifetime. And in the light of an old kerosene lantern, as the children looked on from their beds, they would duel.

Charlie would do "Doin' My Time"—his commentary on marriage—and grin while she stared hard at him from behind her spectacles:

> *On this ol' rock pile*
> *With a ball and chain*
> *They call me by a number*
> *Not my name*

> *Gotta do my time*
> *Lord, Lord*
> *Gotta do my time*

Then Ava would answer with "Wildwood Flower" or something like it:

> *I'll sing and I'll dance*
> *And my laugh shall be gay*
> *I'll charm every heart*
> *And the crowd I will sway*
> *I'll live yet to see him*
> *Regret the dark hour*
> *When he won and neglected*
> *This frail wildwood flower*

And Charlie would sing back at her with another song, about being on a chain gang, or doing time in a Yankee prison, or "All the Good Times Are Past and Gone":

> *I wish to the Lord*
> *I'd never been born*

Or "Knoxville Girl":

> *We went to take an evening walk*
> *About a mile from town*
> *I picked a stick up off the ground*
> *And knocked that fair girl down*

But it always ended in dancing, somehow. He would beat those banjo strings and she would buck-dance around the kitchen, her skirts in her hands, her heavy shoes smacking into the boards, and the children would laugh, because it is impossible not to when your momma acts so young.

* * *

Much, much later, when she had passed seventy, she still played and she still sang but she could not really see how to tune her guitar, and her hand shook too much to do it right, anyway. She would miss a lick now and then, and she would always frown at what time had done to her. But she never forgot the words.

> *I'll think of him never*
> *I'll be wild and gay*
> *I'll cease this wild weeping,*
> *Drive sorrow away*
> *But I wake from my dreaming*
> *My idol was clay*
> *My visions of love*
> *Have all vanished away*

* * *

It didn't all start there, of course, with the beating of that unfortunate woman. The beginning of their story goes way, way back, beyond them, even beyond the first Bundrum to drift here, to these green foothills that straddle the Alabama-Georgia border. In it, I found not only the beginnings of a family history but a clue to our character.

All my life, I have heard the people of the foothills described as poor, humble people, and I knew that was dead wrong. My people were, surely, poor, but they were seldom humble. Charlie sure wasn't, and his daddy wasn't, and I suspect that his daddy's daddy wasn't humble a bit. And Ava, who married into that family, was no wilting flower, either. A little humility, a little meekness of spirit, might have spared us some pain, over the years, but the sad truth is, it's just not in us. With the exception of my own mother, maybe, it never was.

For a family so often poor, we have, for a hundred years or more, refused to adapt our character very much. But then, if we had been willing to change just a little bit, we never would have gotten here in the first place.

We are here because our ancestors were too damn hardheaded to adapt, to assimilate. We are here because someone with a name very much like Bundrum picked a fight with the King of France, and the Church of Rome.

# Run off

*On the Coosa in the 1960s*

AND BACK IN TIME

I was near a fish camp on the Coosa backwater near Leesburg, on the road by Yellow Creek Falls, when I saw my first real buck dance. It was not quite dark, but some fishermen had built a big campfire beside the river and heaved a truck tire on top of it to repel the skeeters. I remember how the oily smoke from the tire wafted over the cattails, how the water had gone black as ink, how glad I was that I was not swimming in it anymore. The tips of spinning rods sprouted from the back of one man's truck, and the doors were wide open, making it easier to hear the radio. It was country, or maybe bluegrass, reedy and scratchy from the speaker, and it serenaded them as they showed off stringers of crappie. It was a scene I had seen so many times that, even though I was still a boy, I almost didn't see it at all. The men had a bottle, and some beer pulled from the same Styrofoam ice chest as the fish, and I stood in the empty parking lot of a bait shop and watched them as I waited for my momma to come out so we could go home. The most I could hope for, I thought as I chunked rocks into the cattails, was to hear some cuss words from the men I had never heard before. Drinking always leads to cussing. Fishing does, too. Or maybe it is merely the absence of wives.

I got a better show than that. One of the men, gaunt, bent and ancient, began to pound on his leg with one fist in rough time to that music. Then, as old, drunk men will, he commenced to dance.

But I had never seen a dance like this. It was not rhythmic, not fluid. The old man stomped hard at the gravel, then shuffled a bit before stomping down hard again, as if he was trying to stamp out fires or snakes. And as he danced he clutched a jelly glass filled with what had to be likker in his hand, and I thought it sure was dumb, because he would only wind up spilling it all over himself. But it was only the bottom part of that old man that was in motion. He held the rest of his body still as a cement angel, his head back, his arms at his sides, as his legs, as if unbidden, did the work. It scared me a little bit.

But it was just buck dancing, about the only kind of dancing my people did. There were no reels, no shags, just this. Folklorists trace it to Ireland and Wales and other places, and it became, over time, the odd ballet that I saw on a riverbank not far from the falls, the stench of burning tires in the wind. I cannot recall the tune, but I can still see that old man banging his bootheels together, spinning, stomping. It was to gentler dancing what a hurtling freight train is to a buggy ride, and it belongs to us, just us. We don't even know how to do it anymore, but it's ours.

Charlie Bundrum was a buck dancer. He had danced it happy, with his work boots skillfully avoiding the tiny feet of laughing girls. And he had danced it sad, lit by a campfire and fresh out of whiskey as his hunting buddy plucked a tune on a Jew's harp. He knew the steps, but he could not have told you where they came from, where they led.

* * *

Charlie could not read. His daddy could not read, and his daddy's daddy could not. There were no old family Bibles in their attics, no giant leather-bound books in which people scribbled an entire family history, listing births, deaths, marriages, war records, baptisms and all the rest. I have seen those books, other people's, littered with yellowed birth certificates, faded blue 4-H Club ribbons and tendrils of lace from hundred-year-old wedding gowns. I always had the feeling that if I shook those Bibles hard enough, the darker, more secret histories would flutter out, too.

My mother kept our memories in a suitcase. It was brown and the size of a portable record player, and it and everything in it burned up in a house fire after I was grown. It had held birth certificates, long letters from my daddy, pictures we drew for her at school, a matchstick cross, vaccination cards, valentines cut from red construction paper, a plaster impression of my right hand, and locks of my baby brother's hair. But it was only about us, and had held no clues to where we came from.

Ava had a family Bible—actually, she had about half a dozen of them. Once, when I sneaked into the dark of her bedroom to go prowling, I opened a massive white leather Bible and found . . . well, I guess I found her. Between the pages were petrified sticks of Juicy Fruit chewing gum, light bills seven years overdue, autographed pictures of Lurleen Wallace, Elvis Presley and Howell Heflin, neatly folded candy bar wrappers, a bill for salvation from Oral Roberts and scraps of prayer, handwritten on the back of envelopes and old Christmas cards. Only Ava would hide prayers in a Bible.

There was no trail here, either. There was no written history. Perhaps, where our family is concerned, there never was. We get some names and dates from army enlistments, marriage records, voting rolls. Only by traveling back through those thin records do we know where we came from, and who the first Bundrum was on this side of the Atlantic, or at least who we believe it was.

Some relatives dispute it, but one thing rings absolutely true: The first Bundrum, if the connection is correct, was just one more poor fool who got run off from someplace else. And being run off, I learned, is a rich family tradition.

Charlie's granddad, James B. Bundrum, who served in the Army of Tennessee, was run off by the Union army. An uncle, John Lewis, was run off by revenuers and didn't stop till he was across the Tennessee River. Charlie's own daddy, Jimmy Jim, was run off by the same revenuers, all the way to south Georgia. In my childhood, men were still being run off.

"Hey, whatever happened to ol' . . . ?" you ask.

"He got run off," someone will say.

"Oh," you say.

Gettin' run off only means you did something bad, and got caught but probably not prosecuted. You can be run off by the rich and powerful, by the government or by hateful women with tiny pistols and no sense of humor.

The first Bundrum—this much we do know—was fleeing something much worse than that.

\* \* \*

His name was not Bundrum but Bondurant, Jean Pierre Bondurant. His journey began in a time of castles and flaming crosses and hanged men, in the din of swords ringing on shields. The events that brought this man to the New World began, if the connection is correct, almost half a millennium ago, as men murdered each other in the name of God. He was a Huguenot.

Wandering people, set adrift by the religious wars of the sixteenth and seventeenth centuries, they were the disenfranchised French Protestants, "walkers of the night," forced to pray in caves, in secret. They had been a strong religious and military force once, which did not endear the sect to Catholics, and it took centuries to beat them down.

In a quest for power in the name of faith, a story as old as the Bible, the two sides fought a bloody civil war, smashing idols and crosses, burning churches, murdering. On August 24, 1572, some thirty thousand Protestants were killed as Catholics took almost total control of the country in the Saint Bartholomew's Day Massacre. Protestants were ostracized, and banned from holding office or respectable jobs.

They were doomed to a life of servitude or starvation, doomed to wander. In some villages the sect was tolerated, but in others its members were beaten, mutilated and hanged. The darkest time was that of Louis XIV, who ushered in an era of nightmare. In 1664 it was decreed that "persons who should speak in public against the doctrines and ceremonies of the Roman religion should be punished by having the lips slit, and the tongue pierced by a hot iron."

That first Bundrum, who did not even know he was one, is no more to us than a name on a ship's passenger manifest. Ship records show that Jean Pierre Bondurant fled to Geneva and then found passage over to England. In late summer of 1700, he boarded the ship *Peter and Anthony,* bound for America. Records show that the ship landed September 20, 1700, in a Huguenot town in Virginia called Manakintowne.

His children and grandchildren—some of them—drifted south, the name Bondurant shifting to Bundren and then Bundrum in deeds, census lists and marriage records. They settled on both sides of the Alabama-Georgia line, voting, marrying, leaving scant records but enough to know they were here, among the first white settlers in these foothills in the beginning of the nineteenth century.

They were farmers. They raised their children on deer meat, salt pork and hoecakes, and pushed ever, ever deeper into the forest of the Southern tribes. The Creeks went to war to stop it, and all but disappeared from the earth. By the middle 1800s, these woods were full of Bondurants, Bundrens, Bundrums and variations of the name.

* * *

The first Bundrum we can put a face to was a gray-bearded, flint-eyed old farm laborer and logger named James B. Bundrum, my grandfather's grandfather, who marched off to fight for the South—and for states' rights, I suppose, because he damn sure didn't own any slaves.

He fought Sherman and U. S. Grant in the up-country as part of the Army of Tennessee, survived camp sickness in the invasion of Kentucky and Yankee sharpshooters in the battle at Chickasaw Bayou, then came home half-starved from the ashes of Georgia to plow a borrowed mule on another man's acreage in Cleburne County in northeastern Alabama.

James B. was husband to Mary Butts, and father to John, William, James, Andy, Sarah, Martha, Louvade and Adiline. Widowed in his old age, he married Sarah Ford and fathered Richard and Monroe. Widowed again, he married Nancy Thompson after the turn of the century when he was near to dying but apparently still inclined to companionship.

He had been poor when he left for the war and he was poor when he came home—what he lost to it was friends, and time. In what Congress had the gall to call "Reconstruction," he labored with the same men that he fought beside, men named Bishop, Hammett, Ingram, Kilgore, Nickson, Shellnutt, Cochran, Butler, Carder, Brown, Cooper, Harrell, Henderson, Hulsey, Jackson, Langley, Moody, Pinkard, Robertson, Childers, Law, Nance, Williams, Wright, Ayers, Caldwell, Camp, Farmer, McGinnis, Morrison, Nickles, Pruitt, Woods, Young, Strickland, Holmes, Kiker, Love, Sanders, Turner and Hamilton, not just names in eroding graveyard granite but names that still live in the thin telephone books and high school football programs here at home. A hundred years later I threw rocks at their descendants across cotton fields and made faces at their great-great-great-granddaughters on the school bus.

They hammered together towns and laid tracks and cut roads, and the designs they carved in this landscape are still here. I have walked railroad trestles they built, crossties rough under my bare feet.

James B. died in 1912. He left no letters and one picture, taken late in his life. It shows a man with eyes like gray marbles and a slash of a mouth set hard and thin above white whiskers that fall halfway down his chest, and his cheeks are grooved and pocked. He is dressed in black clothes and a wide-brimmed hat. He looks like a preacher—but it might have just been Sunday.

What he left behind was children, and they carried the Bundrum name over several counties. His boy James Junior, whom everybody just called Jimmy Jim, was Charlie's father, my mother's grandfather and my great-grandfather.

He was a logger and sawmill hand and a whiskey man, to tell the truth. Lay your hands on the oldest houses in this corner of the world, and you can feel his touch in the wood. He used axes and crosscut saws to fell the trees, and dragged them from the woods with teams of horses. In time, that old-growth timber can get hard as iron, so hard you can bend a sharp nail in it. From what we know of Jimmy Jim, and of his nature, you couldn't drive a nail in him, either.

Him, we know.

But his story, which is Charlie's childhood, almost vanished into the ground with the few very old men and women who remember him, and some of them could not bring him into focus sometimes. They would begin their stories but not always finish them, the same way they used to throw a silver dollar across the Coosa River in, well, sometime, somewhere.

Then I talked to Claude.

\* \* \*

He had lived eighty-six years and begun to talk about dying, not in any self-pitying way but matter-of-fact, the same way he talks about cutting his grass. The two things are inevitable, as Claude Bundrum sees it, two things he has to do sooner or later. Dying would get him out of some yard work, but summer after summer has come and gone and Claude's yard is still just as neat as a widow's closet.

He lives with his wife, Margaret, in a little house on Mountain Avenue in Jacksonville, Alabama, and walks with a cane now, when he goes to visit his sister Myrtle.

"They took out one lung and seven ribs when I was a younger man, and they give up on me that time," said Claude, who is my grandfather's nephew and the last, rickety bridge to Charlie Bundrum's childhood. "When I was eighty-three I had pneumonia, and they give me up that time, too. Now they say I got kidney trouble and . . . Well, a man can't live always."

He remembers his granddad sharp and clear, like a broken bottle. He remembers how everyone walked soft around him, like he was king of the woods.

Like most men, Jimmy Jim was neither all good nor all bad. It is just that when he was bad, gentler people saw in him a disturbing fury. People, a lot of them, don't understand fury. They understand anger and even hatred, but fury is one of those old words that have gone out of style. Jimmy Jim Bundrum understood it. It rode his shoulder like a parrot.

# 3

# Jimmy Jim

*The foothills*

1900–1920

His temper was hot as bird's blood, and his eyes seemed to burn, even in photographs. He had a hooked nose and thick brown mustaches and wore overalls with a black suit coat over them, and was known to carry a little .22 pistol in his coat pocket. He largely disregarded any laws or influence outside his own will, and some people did not like to look him dead in the eye because it made them feel weak. "He was dark-headed, and wasn't scared of the devil," said Claude Bundrum, who grew up in Jimmy Jim's long shadow. "He always drank, and done what he wanted."

But then, there were not many saints working at the end of an ax handle in the woods of Alabama and Georgia, as an era of failed, corrupt reconstruction gave way to a new century.

The history books showed it in black-and-white, and in my mind's eye, as a child, I imagined it that way, a place just too mean for color. I saw a gray landscape under lead-gray sky, where white-robed

Klan rode through dead gray trees, where convicts striped in gray and white swung picks into the bleached, colorless ground, where even the big rivers, in my mind's eye, ran black as tar.

In the text, we read of babies who died of scurvy because oranges cost too much for farmers to afford, and as I read I would imagine a ripe orange, in full color, not merely as an antidote for the scurvy but as an antidote for that whole sorry mess. Even now, when I see oranges, I think about that.

But the foothills were not black, white and gray. They were loud, and green, and often splashed with red, and smelled of manure, and honey, and hot biscuit dough. There were women named Birthannie and mules named Rachel, and about the only things gray were those raggedy uniforms in the attic, which the women cut up and used for quilt scrap.

To the south, where the land flattened out and turned from red to black, there was still a stained white remnant of a plantation culture in the late 1800s and beginning of the 1900s. But here, in the hill country, they would have fed the gentility to their dogs.

Most of the Native Americans who survived the wars were marched out of the foothills at bayonet-point, on a shameful relocation called the Trail of Tears. By the Civil War, the deep woods belonged mostly to white men, but it would be wrong, maybe, to say that what they brought with them was civilization.

Scots, Irish, English and French, men who had starved across the water, came to the foothills to farm, log hardwoods and pine, strip-mine granite, make whiskey, raise kids, hunt deer, breed hunting and fighting dogs, preach, curse and brawl. There were few slaves here because it was too hilly for big cotton—that required good bottomland—so the poor whites did most of the heavy lifting. They were a lot like the Irish who helped settle New Orleans, who came to dig canals and died in heaps from yellow fever because the slaves were just too valuable to waste.

James B. Bundrum, the old rebel soldier, had not left his children much, and few of them could read or write. But in that bare-knuckled culture, his children—and Jimmy Jim, in particular—were at home. They grew in it, the way a weed grows in a crack in a sidewalk.

Born just after the war, Jimmy Jim knew that the carpetbaggers, scalawags and burned-out Southerners would need lumber to rebuild this corner of the South, and he knew that a conquered people would have to drink, to heal or just forget. He could supply their needs.

In the late 1800s, he married the former Mattie Mixon, a gentle woman the people here have long since prayed into heaven. She and Jimmy Jim had seven children together, William, Arthur, Oscar (Babe), Riller, Mag, Charlie and Shuley, in that order. The older children were already grown when Charlie, born in 1907, and then Shuley came along, and their house was often filled with nephews and nieces and cousins, like Claude, Babe's son, who played with Charlie around the ramshackle farmhouse, throwing rocks, climbing trees, buck wild.

Jim did not get rich cutting timber or making whiskey, but made a decent living, and the pasture outside the house was dotted with fat milk cows and the pockets of flatland were streaked with corn rows.

They settled in Websters Chapel, Alabama, which had a reputation back then as a lawless place where men still lived by the feud and their enemies vanished under the leaves. Jim worked his sons hard, taking them to the forest when they were still just little boys. "He put my daddy on the log wagon, and he didn't get off till he was twenty-two," Claude said.

It was brutal work. They hewed railroad crossties by hand, and broke rock in the quarries. Jimmy Jim was less than six feet tall, thin and gaunt, but he had forearms hard as fence posts and could bend a ten-penny nail in his fingers. And when he fought drunk, which was regular, it was terrible. There are many stories of violence attached to the man, but the one people recall most often is the one his grandchildren refer to only as "the finger."

It happened when Charlie was still a boy, around 1915, at a spot in Calhoun County called the Mill Branch, a beautiful clearwater spring where the hard drinkers gathered in the cool of the evening to swap lies and trade dogs and cut each other up a little bit, to settle differences. Rich men would have dueled and said the killing was over honor. Poor men just cut in anger, and sometimes there was honor in it and sometimes the man holding the bloody knife, his mind befuddled from whiskey, just went home and told his wife he reckoned the sheriff would be by, d'rectly.

It wasn't always a killing. Sometimes the men would just beat on each other until their fists bled, not like in Hollywood, but scrambling around on their hands and feet in the gravel, eye-gouging, cussing, mean and wicked in the glow from the massive, popping campfires.

There were so many that the Mill Branch passed into legend. Old drunks are still drawn to that place, and now and then you will pass by there and see one of them sitting quietly in his car, sipping from a can wrapped in a brown paper bag, remembering.

That particular night, as the mules stood tied to the oak trees and the whiskey cooled in the spring, one of the men insulted my great-grandfather, or my great-grandfather imagined he did. He might have just been too drunk to be sure, but he called the man a son of a bitch anyway, and that is usually enough, down here, to pick a fight.

The man was drinking, too, which would have made it a fair fight, if Jimmy Jim knew how to fight fair, which he didn't. They came together inside a yelling ring of onlookers, and it was, by most accounts, a mean and frightful battle. They landed licks that might have killed sober men, kicked at shins and stomped at toes and, it is certain, took the Savior's name in vain over and over again, through mouths that dripped blood.

The man he was fighting, a bigger man, clawed at Jimmy Jim's face and finally got his hands on my great-granddaddy's throat and began with all the strength in his arms and fingers to choke the life out of him. "I couldn't get loose, I couldn't break his holt," Jimmy Jim said later. "I believe he'd of kilt me."

But a man who swings an ax all day has to have arms like iron and fingers like rivets, and Jimmy Jim slowly prised one of the man's fingers from his throat, then another and another. But then the man hooked one of his fingers, maybe two, inside Jimmy Jim's cheek, and just hauled back on it, tearing at the flesh, making Jim howl in agony. The man was trying to rip his cheek out, so Jimmy Jim did what he had to do.

He bit off one of the man's fingers at the second joint.

It was not a clean bite, and witnesses said he had to gnaw a bit to get it done. The man started to wail, and my great-granddaddy spit and that was by God that. He just stood there, with blood running down his mouth, and grinned as the man sank to his knees, whimpering, holding his bloody hand.

History is unclear as to which finger it was—it was too big to be the pinky, everyone agrees—or from which hand it was gnawed, but we know precisely what happened to it. Jimmy Jim took the finger home in the pocket of his overalls, and placed it on the mantel.

Mattie, it is told, left the dreadful thing there on her mantel until Jimmy Jim sobered up, and then threw it in the yard, where it was snatched up by a chicken.

If there was any softness in Jimmy Jim, it was held prisoner by the place, the culture and a closed mind. Mattie suffered.

She was a small and humble woman who, weak from childbirth and crippled after her hip was shattered by a cow, worked herself to death. But behind her husband's back she told her children long stories, sang songs that Charlie remembered a lifetime, and, even as she grew weaker, paler, thinner, she made her children laugh. She made up stories about the forest and the possums, wildcats, deer and bears that held Charlie and the other children rapt, stories better than any book, better than stories about beanstalks and such. Years later, when

Charlie told them late in the evenings to his own children, it was Mattie they heard.

"She was an awful good woman," Claude said.

Charlie, her second-youngest, grew up to be his daddy's son, yes, a whiskey man, brawler and all of it, but Mattie saved her boy just as surely as if she had stomped to death a serpent at his feet.

Charlie did what his daddy told him, worked when he was told, and spent his days watching, learning. But as a man, when he talked about his family and that time, his daddy was just a name, but his momma was a bird flying.

* * *

But as his momma taught him how to live, his daddy taught him how to stay alive. It was a time when the men still taught the woods to their sons, and Charlie learned from the best.

Jimmy Jim moved like a shadow through the forest, his hob-nailed boots soft as velvet slippers in the dry leaves. He and his brothers, all woodsmen, taught their sons how to get so close to a deer even a five-dollar rifle could not miss, taught them how to run a trotline and bait it cheap, with rank meat or stale bread, because catfish are just naturally stupid and a man would not waste a good worm on them. He taught his sons not to fear a scream in the night, even the panthers. He would take them into the woods and, when the cats screamed, grab their hands in a bone-crushing grip and hold them in place as the soft pad of feet passed. The little boys would jerk, pull and wail, but old Jim held tight, teaching.

The old women, witch women and sin eaters said the panthers were not really animals but devils, and hounds would go crazy on their chains and the porch dogs would hide under the house when the screams started. Jimmy Jim didn't give a damn. He would saddle his horse and load his 12-gauge and ride off into the night, not in search of panthers but to tend his still.

Jimmy Jim made likker quietly on both sides of the state line in northern Georgia and Alabama, augmenting his sawmill and logging income, running off gallon after gallon and fooling the law, mostly, for decades in the late 1800s and early 1900s. It was a family business. His brother, John Lewis, was in it, and they worked at it together until the revenuer men ran John Lewis clear up to the Tennessee River.

That happened in 1891, in what family members still refer to as "the trouble." John Lewis Bundrum was minding a still in Cleburne County when a revenuer, a federal man, surprised him. John Lewis vaulted on his mule and put the heels to him, but the revenuer was better mounted, and was slowly, slowly gaining.

John Lewis reined in, stepped calmly down off the mule, drew a rifle from a tow sack, took careful aim and shot the revenuer's horse, which effectively ended any pursuit.

It was a Christian gesture—toward the revenuer, not the horse—but he would have been better off shooting the revenuer. He would not have been missed that much, revenuers being about as popular as itch.

But a good horse is a good horse, and they might have hung him if he had not fled to the north, to Florence up on the Tennessee River. That seemed far enough, being almost in Tennessee. When he came home, almost a year later, he found that his wife had died of typhoid fever. Heartbroke, he left Alabama for Arkansas, and he is buried there, in Benton.

If there was a lesson in what happened to John Lewis, his little brother, Jimmy Jim, failed to see it.

By the time Charlie Bundrum was ten years old, his daddy was as well known for his likker as for his lumber. Jimmy Jim took Charlie to the woods with him to help carry the whiskey out, tote wood and watch out for revenuers. Before he was even a teenager, Charlie knew how the corn fermented into mash and how the pure, pale likker was distilled a potent, precious drop at a time. It was in his blood a long, long time before he ever took his first drink of it.

Over time, Jimmy Jim left his older boys to do the lumber work and spent more and more time at his stills. The federal men and county deputies began to find them and when they did they poured out his mash and used axes to bust up his copper plumbing. Soon he was a wanted man. In the north Georgia mountains, they surprised him at his still but he lost them in the brush after some shooting, but no serious shooting.

But the deputies and the federal men started watching his house and watching the roads, so he couldn't come home, couldn't see his wife and children. He went into hiding down in the flatland in south Georgia, as his small wealth dwindled, as his family suffered.

He would hop a freight train or bum a ride and get off when he was close to Rome, and creep up to his door in the dead of night. But with papers out on him, he had to stay gone for years, and the little bit of money he was able to leave did not help much.

When Charlie was twelve, Mattie's hip was crushed by a kicking milk cow, and, her husband being a fugitive, there was no money for a doctor or hospital. The bones grew back wrong and she was deformed and lame, a woman who moved the rest of her life by swinging her whole body side to side. They lived in a shack. Their one salvation was that Jimmy Jim had left them with a few milk cows, and even though Mattie was crippled, she milked and churned butter. That, and charity, kept them alive.

Riller, who was grown then and married to Tobe Morrison, a steel worker with a good job, came to the house one day and took the youngest, Shuley, to live with them. Kinfolks refer to it as "the day Riller stole little Shuley," but they know she did it to feed him, to help.

Charlie went to work for himself. He took a little wagon up into the woods, searching for pine stumps. He hacked them into sections, what folks here call knots, and sold them door to door for pennies. People used the slivers from the fat pine to start their fire. He swung an ax like a man and did any odd job he could find. He grew up that way, hard, but at night, if she wasn't in too much pain, he and his momma talked until the fire burned out. I would like to have heard what they said. But I guess the words don't matter all that much.

There are few photographs of that time, but one, if you look at it hard and long enough, tells the story pretty well. It was taken when he was still a boy, during bad times.

The photo's backdrop is a ragged shack of rough, unpainted board and the windows, without glass, are covered by a flap of black tar paper. The poverty is burned deep into the print. But the boy in the foreground is not one of those pitiful, hollow-eyed urchins who stare up from photo books of the Appalachians. Instead, he has a faint, almost imperceptible smile, as if the hard-eyed kinfolks who pose with him just haven't heard the joke yet.

His sister Riller, already grown and married, stands beside him, her severe face framed by a black cloth hat. Someone has strung a garland of flowers, on a string or a vine, and looped it over the crown.

\* \* \*

Mattie died at fifty-four, when Charlie was barely fifteen, and her children buried her in the pretty graveyard at Mount Gilead Church, in Websters Chapel. Hills rise up from the cemetery on almost every side, creating deep shade around the church. It is a lovely place to rest, that little pocket of cool, quiet dark.

Charlie never, ever talked about the funeral, about his momma in death, so I don't know what was said, what was done for her. But in time I would learn that it is a tradition with us. We blot out the funeral—we erase the image of the coffin and the flowers and even the prayers—or at least we try. It is as if the dead just walked off somewhere, just after leaving us with a story, or a covered dish, or a whittled toy.

I have always said my people are smart.

* * *

By his momma's death, Charlie was more man than most ever get, a tall, hard, strong and smiling man, as if he were immune to the fires that had scorched him, if not purified by them.

He lived for fiddle music and corn likker, and became a white-hot banjo picker and a buck dancer and a ladies' man, because women just love a man who can dance. At seventeen he could cut lumber all day, then tell stories all night, and people in the foothills said he would never settle down or maybe even amount to much. But the boy could charm a bird off a wire. And there seemed to be no fear in him, no fear at all. It was almost as if he had died already, met the devil and knew he could charm him or trick him or even whip him, because what did ol' Scratch have left to show him that he had not already seen.

* * *

His daddy was an upright citizen, toward the end.

The warrants for Jimmy Jim's arrest had all faded to yellow, and he came home from the flat country to marry again, this time to a pretty nineteen-year-old girl named Ruth. But little Ruth died less than a year later in childbirth, and he buried her with the baby, an unnamed girl child, in a grave in Georgia, the still infant resting in her rigid arms.

No one seems to know why the lawmen in the foothills, on either side of the state line, let him be. It may be he was older, and seen as less dangerous. It may be they just forgot him. He went to work making coffins, and traveled, visiting his children and grandchildren.

It is mostly a myth, I believe, that men will mellow with time—

there are men in my family who would hack off your ear as they waited to die in the nursing home—but Jimmy Jim seemed to change, to bend, I guess.

I heard from my momma that he would go to his children's houses and teach their wives how to make stew. He met my grandma, Ava, and Ava, hard to impress, said late in her own life that she liked the old man.

It may be, as some said, he just felt hell licking at his ankles and tried to change. It happens a lot, down here. It is why a lot of the deacons are old men. But Jimmy Jim was not used up, not quite yet. At sixty-two, he married Dolee Semmes Fowler, and soon she was expecting a child.

\* \* \*

He had been a dramatic man all his life. But on February 15, 1927, his heart just stopped. It would have been more befitting his legend if Jimmy Jim had been shot down in a pistol fight. But he went out soft and quiet, like a cat leaving a room.

They buried him in north Georgia, in the high mountains near Chattanooga. His last child, Vera, was born after his death.

\* \* \*

In the spring of 1994, a tornado, the storm of the century, tore across the mountain and dropped onto the Mount Gilead cemetery, knocking some of the headstones over and pulling others from the ground. Mattie's headstone was untouched.

# 4.

# Whistle britches

*The foothills*

THE 1920S

He could run, man, could he run. Up and over the ridges and down, down into the hollows, he trailed the dogs that trailed the possums, his ears tuned to their music. The hounds would bark short and sharp as they ran through the darkness, their miraculous noses scudding along the pine needles and dead leaves, seeking, seeking, all the time gaining, gaining. Charlie ran with a tow sack trailing his back pocket, swinging a lantern from one fist, and in the pitch black of the woods it looked like a ball of lightning bouncing through the brush and trees. Then the timbre of the music would change, from the quick, static barks to an urgent, mournful howl, and Charlie would shout out "Treed!" to the men who were too old or fat or drunk to keep up, and he'd follow that sound to the dogs. The hounds, their ears half chewed away from encounters with angry coons and bobcats, would be quivering and baying and staring up into the dark branches, doing what they were bred to do. The possum, silver-gray with teeth that could punch a

47

hole in a can of Pet milk, would hiss from his perch, his eyes shining red in the gloom.

"Got you, Mr. Possum," Charlie would say, and he'd climb up and deftly snatch that possum by the scruff and stick it in a sack.

"Let the dogs have him," some men would say, wanting to see some sport. But Charlie, still a teenager then, would just shake his head.

"They's a colored lady in town gives me fifty cents," he'd say, and he would drag the dogs away from the trees—a good hunting dog is smart but will fixate on a tree the way some men fixate on lost love—and get them running down another trail, to another possum.

If he couldn't sell them, he would give them away and hope to be invited for supper—hopefully on a night they were not having possum.

Later, the men would gather around a fire and tell lies and stories, and to Charlie that was as good as anything on this earth.

The most famous such story from his time was that of a man who sat by the fire lamenting that his wife was not a beautiful woman.

"Beauty," one of the hunters told him, "is skin deep."

The man thought about that a minute.

Then he got up and walked off into the darkness.

"Where you a'goin'?" someone shouted after him.

"Home," came his voice, from the darkness. "To skin my wife."

These are the stories young Charlie heard and told as he hunted, fished and loafered from Georgia to Alabama and back again in the first two decades of the twentieth century, moving by car, mule wagon or passing freight car. Some people say poverty is a box. For Charlie, as a teenager, it was everything outside the box.

He was as free as a man could be, with no land, no money, just a borrowed bed in some kinfolks' houses and a change of clothes. He could have tied everything he owned to the end of a stick, asked someone to feed his dog and hopped a train, leaving this place for good.

But this was his place, even though he did not own enough of it to fill a snuffbox. It was his as much as anybody's.

Him and his kind were too wild for church and too raggedy for the Kiwanis Club, but they were as much a part of the landscape as the mockingbirds and the camellias and the red brick—baked from the clay—that held up the towns.

They lived on mostly beans and bread, but it was good beans, good bread. On every stove, a pot of pintos simmered, a ham hock or a thick piece of fatback swimming in the thick brown soup. They ate great northerns, limas, black-eyed peas and purple butter beans, but nothing even came close to pinto beans. Pintos were good enough for company.

In every stove, a golden cake of cornbread baked in an iron skillet, and the smell of the hot bread and bacon grease—you always smeared bacon grease around the skillet before you poured in the meal—would draw people in from the yard. The women would put the pone of bread on a dinner plate and cover the top with another dinner plate, because that's how it was always done and always will be.

Sometimes, if the season was right, the women would mix pork cracklin's—little cubes of rendered pork fat and skin—into the meal and lard and buttermilk or water, and men carried it—just that—in their lunch pails to the cotton mills, coal mines and pipe shops.

And sometimes, for a change, people just crumbled up a little cornbread in a glass or a bowl and poured cold buttermilk or sweet milk over it, and ate it with a spoon. They chopped hot Spanish onions up in it, and that was a meal.

They fried okra and squash and green tomatoes in the summer, and turned cucumbers into sweet pickles and pickled cabbage and pepper sauce into chow-chow, a red-hot relish that people ate with their beans. In the fall they ate collards and cooked turnips with butter and salt and pepper—a good turnip will just melt under your tongue. Deer rode across the hoods of Model Ts and across the rumps of mules, and smart cooks ground it up with a little pork sausage, to give it taste, or soaked roasts in buttermilk, to make the meat less gamey. They scrambled squirrel brains into their eggs, and made candy for their children by melting cane sugar in skillets and then letting it get hard.

They lived in tightly packed mill villages where the sturdy little houses, all exactly the same but all with a real front porch, seemed so much better than anything they had ever lived in before. Or, like Charlie's kin, they stayed in the woods in ramshackle houses that had never seen a coat of paint.

They rented, because they were one class below the owners, and owning land was a dream that most of them certainly had. But it might as well have been a dream about steamships and zeppelin rides, for all it would amount to, for generations.

But there was a dignity in them that no amount of servitude could collapse. The women wore their hair long—dictated by the doctrine of a Protestant faith—and the men, even the young ones like Charlie, draped their overalls in severe black coats for court and funerals and voting. A man has to have a lot of dignity to walk around proud with most of the rear end worn out of his overalls. But a pair of ventilated breeches, Charlie figured, was no reason to bow your head.

* * *

By the time he was fully grown, Charlie stood more than six feet tall but weighed less than one hundred and sixty pounds. When he climbed into his faded blue overalls, he looked like a mast stuck in a sail. "Whistle britches," old men would say, grinning, because of the breeze that surely found a way into his clothes through the ragged holes or flapping pants legs.

It was the seat that always wore out first, because he found work as a roofer early on, and the shingles, like sandpaper, just ate the cloth away as he skidded around the roof on his rump and knees. His sisters sewed patches on the inside of his overalls, for decency's sake.

He wore the same thing every day, because it was all he had. In the winter he wore long underwear under his Liberties, and a canvas work shirt that might have been some color once, but now was gray. He wore lace-up leather boots, what people called hobnails, strung with thin strips of leather, because cloth rotted in the weather, and he wore them when he was working, fishing and dancing. Men like him wore their hobnails to funerals under black suits. They got married in them, and worked saddle soap or oil into the leather to keep it from cracking. When the boots finally wore out, they threw them to a hound puppy, which gnawed them down to the bootheel, then nothing. They came from Lehigh, Pennsylvania, and they cost a week's pay, so a man had to get the good out of them.

He was bareheaded only when he ate and slept, otherwise wearing a denim cap low down over his brow, so that his eyes, which had a natural shine, looked like headlights in a tunnel. The cap, like everything else, wore out from the weather and dry rot, and his hair stuck through it. People smiled at that, too. Stick a punkin' on his head, and prop him there in the corn, they joked, to scare the crows and coons away.

He didn't own a watch. The boss man told him when to come, go and eat his lunch, which was biscuit and cornbread, mainly. He was sixteen, going on seventeen, gangly, gaunt, with air-conditioned pants.

But if you looked down, down to the ends of those skinny arms, you could see signs of the man's character—the man the boy would be—in his hands.

Not the arms. His arms were abnormally long, with long muscles from real work, but so narrow and thin that his elbows stuck out like onions. Just the hands.

The hands were magnificent.

They hung at the ends of his skinny arms like baseball mitts, so big that a normal man's hand disappeared in them. The calluses made an unbroken ridge across his palm, and they were rough, rough all over, as shark's skin. The grease and dirt, permanent as tattoos, inked his skin, and the tar and dirt colored the quick under his fingernails, then and forever. He could have burned his overalls, changed his name and bought himself a suit and tie, but those hands would have told on him.

And they were strong, finger-crushing, freakishly strong, as if the tendons in his arms were steel cables that worked a machine made to kink pipe, crush rocks and pull stumps. He could grip a man's wrist and squeeze—just squeeze—and make his eyes water.

When he would tell a story, he would clamp one big hand down on his listener's leg, at about the knee, and—especially if he had been nipping a little bit—squeeze to make a point. Grown men would wince, cuss and howl. But he always got to finish his story.

In a fight, and there were some, he clenched his fingers in a fist the size of a baking hen, and it was like being hit in the face with a pine knot.

But that was just sideshow stuff. The hammer seemed to dance in his hand, and he was twice as fast—machine-gun fast—as most men on the rooftops, slapping down shingles, pounding them in place. His daddy, Jimmy Jim, had strong hands like that, agile hands. Charlie got them from him.

After work, the big hands with the long fingers could pick out beautiful notes on the banjo, which he learned from his kinfolks. When Charlie visited them, he would sit a baby on its bottom in one big hand and just stare into its face, until it gurgled or grinned or squalled. He wasn't rough with them, and he liked to hold them.

* * *

Few doors were closed to him, because of his nature. Sober, he was a fine listener. Drunk, he hogged the very air. He spoke in the language—the very specific language—of the Appalachian foothills. It was an unusual mix of formal English and mountain dialect. The simple word "him" was two distinct sounds—"he-yum." And a phrase like "Well, I better go," was, in the language of our people, more likely to sound like "Weeeellllll, Ah bet' go." Some words are chopped off and some are stretched out till they moan, creating a language like the terrain itself. Think of that language as a series of mountains, cliffs, valleys and sinkholes, where only these people, born and raised here, know the trails.

Charlie spoke with a smooth, low voice. If he wanted to make a point, he just said damn, for punctuation, as in "That's a damn big house, fellers, to roof in this damn heat."

He did not curse in front of ladies, usually, and among men he drew a line between good, solid biblical cursing and what he called "ugly talk," which was anything a twelve-year-old would scrawl on an outhouse wall.

He did not spit in front of ladies, even if he had to swallow the juice. He tipped his hat, like in a cowboy matinee.

* * *

He was blessed with that beautiful, selective morality that we Southerners are famous for. Even as a boy, he thought people who steal were trash, real trash. He thought people who would lie were trash.

"And a man who'll lie," he said, even back then, "will steal."

Yet he saw absolutely nothing wrong with downing a full pint of likker—a full pint is enough to get two men drunk as lords—before engaging in a fistfight that sometimes required hospitalization.

He saw no reason to obey some laws—like the ones about licenses, fees and other governmental annoyances—but he would not have picked an apple off another man's ground and eaten it.

\* \* \*

He was not literate, but he was no fool. He could figure in his head the carpenter's calculations needed to roof a house or build one—some men just have a gift that way—but while men came to respect him for his abilities, he would always be the one who did their lifting for them.

If they talked down to him, he quit and he never worked for them again. The South of Charlie Bundrum had a strict class system, and he was beholden to the monied whites for his living. But even as a boy he thought his life was worth just as much as anyone else's. "We're as good as anybody," he liked to say. It might have been obvious, as he rode past in a ragged car, a big tar bucket on the floorboards, that some people lived better. But if there was any envy, it never boiled up to where it passed his lips. He did not hate a rich man, did not covet his life, at least that anyone can remember.

He did not talk about heaven, the way a lot of poor people did then and always will, to justify their struggle on this earth.

He was funny that way.

He was happy being who he was, without even an expectation of wings, and feet of clay.

\* \* \*

If someone, maybe around a fire on one of those riverbanks, had asked him then, "What do you want, Charlie," he could have told them.

He wanted enough work to live decent, and on a Saturday he wanted a drink of likker, because it sent the silver shivers down him and that was good.

He wanted a ham and biscuit. He wanted to hear some music,

and watch a pretty girl walk down the street in town, if he could do it and not be obvious about it.

He wanted, even though he was just a boy himself, some babies. His heart melted around them, his spirit soared. He might not have been able to put it into words, but they made him noble, they raised him up.

And he wanted that little four-eyed gal, the one he had seen at a basketball game over by Gadsden on the Alabama side. There was just something about a black-haired girl with blue eyes.

Claude Bundrum, his kin, knew Ava Hamilton when she was a young woman. He knew that, even then, she was different—if not outright peculiar.

"And meeting Charlie," he said, "probably didn't help things none."

# 5.

# Four-Eyes

God made just one.

In size, she wasn't much, just a little thing, a tad bowlegged, with hair down past her waist and those startling, silver-blue eyes. But the Maker must have had some personality left over from somebody else—Lutherans maybe—because He gave Ava about twice as much as anybody else. Even when she was growing up on her daddy's nice farm in the Alabama foothills, her anger burned hotter and her happiness flashed brighter, it seemed, than was altogether natural. When sorrow gripped her, it gripped her like barbed wire, and her wails would make a person shiver. But when she was happy she drew everyone around her into the circle of her warmth, her joy, and you were grateful for it even as you waited for the mood to sharply turn, like a Sunday drive that ends in a head-on collision.

Her eyes went weak early in life, and she had to wear wire-rimmed glasses to read. People would drive past the house and wave at the little girl on the porch with a book or a newspaper in her hands, but she didn't look up. She loved learning, people said, and if it had been another time or place Ava might have been anything, done anything. But love, and luck, set her walking down a different road.

Ava's momma, Mary Matilda, believed that being in the country was no excuse for being dumb as a turnip, and wanted her children to read. She bought them books, and got the newspaper mailed in from Atlanta, only a day or so late.

Ava loved that newspaper. She read it and reread it. It brought the assassination of Archduke Ferdinand and the Battle of Verdun and the fight in the Argonne Forest. In those pages, zeppelins fell from the sky and burst into flames and Pancho Villa invaded the United States on horseback. It may have seemed like it was just a little girl with glasses sitting on a porch with a paper in her lap in rural Alabama, but the whole world spun around her there on the front porch when the paper came.

Her father, William Alonzo Hamilton, was a hard-bitten Congregational Holiness, and convinced that the only book worth reading was the King James Bible. He had built a self-sustaining farm outside Gadsden in Etowah County, the kind of farm you see on Christmas cards, and even as Mary Matilda weaned her children on music and poetry, he fed them a steady diet of hard work and hard-rock religion.

There was, besides Ava, George, Bill, Fred, Grace, Lula, Plummer and Ruth, and on Sunday they filled half a pew. Ava learned her Bible forward and backward and sideways. She could tell you how long Moses wandered and how long Job suffered with sores and what fate befell Lot's wife and what Paul and Silas had to do with things in general.

The Congregational Holiness take their Bible straight up, and if you have never seen a Holiness service, do not go if you expect it to be like any other Protestant faith. Ava grew up in a faith where the people get happy and just start to yell, where people begin to speak in tongues, fall out on the floor and weep and laugh and go into trances, as if dead. God does not tiptoe into a Congregational Holiness church, He busts down the door and raises the roof and, quick as death, He is among them.

"They was shoutin' people," my mother, Margaret, told me. "Grace always said they was Baptists but they wasn't Baptists because Baptists don't shout. That much."

The Hamiltons had roots, deep roots, in the foothills, and were, for lack of a better word, respectable. The children went to school and Ava was even a cheerleader at Ashville School. When she was in her eighties, she would break into a cheer sitting on the edge of the bed, then just lay back and go to sleep.

The schools in the foothills after the turn of the century did not have football teams, but many of them had small gymnasiums or hard asphalt courts, and on Friday nights boys played basketball in shining satin uniforms and black high-top tennis shoes. It was a time of two-handed set shots and granny-style free throws, but it was entertaining, and people came to games in wagons or on muleback. Men in overalls talked cotton prices and mule genealogy as Daughters of the Confederacy sold soft drinks for a nickel, and somebody always had a jug in the parking lot, if that's what you call a place where the conveyances had to be roped tight to posts to keep them from running off.

Ava's school, Ashville, was the bitterest rival of neighboring Steele Station, and the opposing team's cheerleaders would taunt them with:

> *Chew tobaccer*
> *Chew tobaccer*
> *Spit, spit, spit*
> *Ashville, Ashville*
> *Thinks they're it*

And the Ashville cheerleaders would stomp their feet and answer with:

> *Steele Station*
> *Starvation*
> *Sorriest place*
> *In creation*

Ava made good grades without trying a lick, but what she was really gifted at was music. Passersby came to remark on how, every time they drove their mule wagons past the Hamilton farm, it was as if someone had opened the lid on God's own music box.

> *I heard an old, old story*
> *How a Savior came*
> *From glory*
> *How He gave his life*
> *On Calvary*
> *To save a wretch like me*

The music was everywhere, in the barn, in the fields of tomatoes and okra, out in the tall cotton, serenading the chickens, appeasing the pigs. It was almost like it was in the ground itself, but it was only in the children.

Ava and her brothers and sisters sang and played music because it was just so easy for them, the way other people are just tall, or fat, or redheaded. Not one of them was tone-deaf or all thumbs. Ava sang hymns to the corn rows and beasts of the field in a voice, I am told, of angels.

> *Victory in Jesus*
> *My Savior, forever*

*He sought me, and bought me*
*With His redeeming blood*

Sweet tenor and rich baritone drifted from the porch, and guitar pickers traded licks under the trees, plucking out gospel and bluegrass and even, when their daddy wasn't looking, a little white man's blues—stolen by William Alonzo's boys when they snuck off to the train station in Gadsden. They risked hard whippings and eternal damnation to hear the raggedy whiskey drinkers pick on beat-up Gibsons before some deputy told them to just move on down the road.

The girls sang sweet and high at the clothesline, in the squash rows, with hoes in their hands. It was in them, and had to come out. Ava's favorite was "Victory in Jesus," but she loved "Birmingham Jail," and "Precious Memories," and "The Wreck of the Old 97," and, especially, "Wabash Cannonball."

*Oh, listen to the jingle*
*The rumble and the roar*
*As she glides across the woodlands*
*Through the hills and by the shore*
*Hear the mighty rush of the engine*
*Hear the lonesome hoboes call*
*You're traveling through the jungle on*
*The Wabash Cannonball*

Ava Hamilton was a Presley on her momma's side, and was, in fact, a far distant relative of Elvis, though we have never tried to claim any of his money. The Presleys were musical people, singers and pickers, and that is where the gift came from. Mary Matilda played hymns on the piano and organ and taught her children how to read notes, how to play everything.

But Ava did not have to read notes. She could hear a song on the

Victrola or the Philco and sit down at the piano or snatch up a banjo or guitar and just play, and strangers were amazed. She just knew which key or which string matched the sound she had heard.

The only thing she could not do was play the violin, or fiddle. She tried, and the sound that came out could not be described as music. She would get mad, put it down and go pound hard on the piano. She had, most of her childhood, a harmonica hidden in the folds of her dress—seventy years later, she still did—and she would draw it like a gun and play:

> *Goin' up Cripple Creek*
> *Goin' in a run*
> *Goin' up Cripple Creek*
> *To have some fun*

\* \* \*

This was a whole other culture than the one Charlie Bundrum was raised in, even though the people shared space beneath the same forest, traveled the same dirt roads. But one, his, was a culture of stills and eye-gouging fistfights and riverbank campfires where men passed clear whiskey from hand to hand and could cuss like champions. The other one, hers, was one where a woman taking off her bonnet in mixed company would make tongues wag.

Charlie and Ava saw each other for the first time, it is believed, at one of those basketball games. But they did not meet, formally, until the box-lunch social in Gadsden some months later.

At the socials, girls of courting age would fix a box lunch and boys of courting age, and sometimes old men who had been widowed, would bid on the food—but of course what they were really buying there was the pleasure of the young woman's company for the time it took to eat.

Ava's box lunch was, it must be said, a little bit of a lie. She was no great cook as a young woman and her sisters had actually done the entire meal, figuring that Ava would never get married if she poisoned a man to death. So they fried some chicken and boiled some eggs and put in a wedge of pound cake, and dressed Ava in a pretty cotton dress with red flowers on it, and a matching bonnet. Then they tucked the box under Ava's arm and eased her onto the stage, where fate and Charlie found her.

Later, when the fiddling started, someone laid down some boards and they buck-danced to the music, but they got a little off track and tore up the grass.

The fiddler was an old man who knew songs from Ireland, Scotland and Wales, but now and then he would break into something written by and for these people, songs about mountain railroads and young love under willow trees and sometimes, as Ava would say, just plain folly.

> *I got a pig at home in a pen*
> *Corn to feed him on*
> *All I need is a pretty little girl*
> *To feed him when I'm gone*

And it suited Miss Hamilton and Mr. Bundrum to stomp, eyes locked on each other, till the band stopped playing.

He had few prospects. Her daddy didn't think much of him. His reputation, for drinkin' and flirtin' and fightin', was not good, even, Old Man Hamilton surmised, for Baptists. Ava's family just said no to Charlie Bundrum and sent him away, and figured he would disappear.

He did.

They both did.

\* \* \*

They lied about their age and got a preacher named Jones to marry them in his house in Gadsden, when she was sixteen and he was seventeen. And Ava just walked away from the upstanding, church-going life she had been raised in and followed a boy, a boy who could not even read or write, into uncertainty.

He just went and stole her out of it really, because he felt he deserved something special, and she went with him because she felt she did, too.

# 6.

# In the wild

*On the Oostanaula, the Coosa and the Etowah*

THE 1920S

The men had been drinking the evening Jeff Baker got stabbed and bled clean through the brown sugar, his hot blood melting it, turning it into treacle just as fast as Newt Morrison and Mr. Hugh Sanders could pack it in his wounds. Jeff moaned and trembled, and the men praised God that Jeff had so much good likker in him, because surely that numbed his pain and prepared his soul.

It was in the summer, not long after they were wed, on the river not far from Newt Morrison's farm. Newt, Mr. Hugh, Charlie, Jeff and some other men had walked down to the river to a still, to have a taste. The women—Ava, Newt's daughter, Sis, and some others—sat on a wide porch, visiting.

As soon as the men were pretty well stone-blind, Jeff, a big man in his twenties who had no visible means of support and was also rumored to be unparticular about which chicken coop he visited late at night, got into a fistfight with a man about as big as his leg. Jeff beat him into a bloody heap on the ground, but the little man was a gamer, and kept on coming.

Finally the small man staggered to his feet for what all the men there hoped would be the last time, and Jeff, who was not an evil man at heart, waved a fist at him to stay away, and turned his back.

Somewhere in his clothes the little man found a pocketknife, and he jumped on Jeff's back and snaked one arm hard around his throat. Then he just started stabbing, reaching over to plunge the blade into Jeff's side and chest, the knife like a windmill, flinging drops of blood.

Jeff was screaming, staggering. The other men—they might have acted faster if they had not been so damned drunk—pulled the tiny man off him and flung him aside, and Jeff slumped face first in the dirt.

"He's kilt," Newt said, as the little man ran off, crashing through the weeds.

But the wounds still pumped blood. The men all grabbed an arm or leg and staggered—from the weight of the man, and their own unsteady, tossing decks—all the way back to Newt's house. Newt called for brown sugar. Everyone knew that if you packed a wound with enough brown sugar, it could clot the blood and stop a man from bleeding to death.

But as fast they could cake it on, the blood from the stab wounds washed it away, until Newt and Mr. Hugh were bloody up to their elbows and most of the people had begun to pray. Mr. Hugh searched his mind for a scripture that could save the man. Just because a man is drunk does not mean he cannot speak to the Lord.

"Does anybody know that goddamn Bible verse?" he shouted. "This son of a bitch is bleeding to death."

"Which 'un?" several people asked.

"Ezekiel," he yelled.

Ava, who hated any violence she was not directly involved in, had stood trembling. But now she stepped smartly forward as if called from on high, and knelt at the man's side.

"And when I passed by thee, and see thee polluted in thine own blood," she quoted, "I said unto thee, 'When thou wast in thy blood, live ye.' I said unto thee, 'When thou wast in thy blood, live.' "

"That 'un," Mr. Hugh said, looking at Ava in something close to awe.

"Chapter 16," Ava said.

Mr. Hugh said that seemed like it.

"Verse 6," Ava said.

It would be a grand story if the blood had ceased to flow right then, at that precise moment, but it didn't. Yet somehow, either through the will of God or the coagulating properties of brown sugar, the wounds soon stopped pouring and began to seep, slowly. Of course, by then Jeff was bled almost white.

They figured there was no need to take him to a doctor, and when he came to he told them, "No, I reckon I'll just lay here and die."

He paid Sis and Newt's other children a nickel a day to brush the flies off him, and he waited to die for a long, long time. Finally, after a few days, Newt told him that if he wasn't going to die he sure did want his porch back, and Jeff got up and walked on down the road.

\* \* \*

This was the life Charlie had delivered Ava unto, a place where people still lived shrouded by the trees, where the local sheriff was a deacon who meted out justice based on the season, because all the roads in and out of the backcountry were dirt and his old Model T was bad to sink up to its axles in the mud. Here, the people knew, a man sometimes just needed killing, and if it was more or less unanimous, the kilt man was buried quietly and no one ever saw any reason to call the law.

Here, Ava would need every scrap of Bible she ever knew.

She was not a city girl. Ava had been raised with a hoe in her hand, swatting at sweat bees, and she had stood on the fence and gazed unblinking when her daddy entered their hogpen with a .22 rifle and a razor-sharp butcher knife. But the place Charlie took her to was not safe and solid country living the way she had known it.

Charlie took her to a high place in Georgia, cut by three rivers. In Rome, smack-dab in the middle of that city, the Etowah and the Oostanaula converged to form the Coosa, and it was the Coosa that, all his life, ran through Charlie's heart.

Rome bustled with cotton mills, cement plants and ironworks that specked the night sky with orange fires. It had a massive drawbridge down on Fifth Avenue that opened to let the barges through. Endless trains, hauling tons of iron ore, belched smoke and shook the earth. Children put pennies on the tracks and the weight mashed them thin as notebook paper.

Most roads were dirt and brick, but the place had a clock tower so high that it disappeared from sight on a cloudy day, and a brand-new federal courthouse, lousy with revenuers.

Charlie didn't much like town, but the industry meant workers and workers meant houses, and a good hammer swinger could make a living here. But like many men who had grown up in the woods, he saddled his mule and rode off into the trees when the boss man said quit, and he did not stop until the foundry fires were lost in the distance and the ground did not shake from machines.

The river ran there, right there. The Coosa, a muddy green where it ran clean and swift around giant rocks, turned brown when the red mud washed in from the rains. The river flooded high, clean up into the low branches of trees. It ate into the banks and formed deep caves overhung by the twisted, exposed roots of trees that clung to the disappearing ground.

Monsters lived here. Fat water moccasins coiled around the lower branches, thick as a man's arm. Snapping turtles, as big around as a car tire with jaws strong enough to snap a broomstick in two, lurked in the deep, dark holes. Just under the river's surface, primeval catfish, four feet long, hung suspended in that translucent water as their whiskers, like snakes clinging to their jaws, undulated in the slow current.

Charlie spent every spare moment on it. He did not have a store-bought boat. He took the hoods of two junk cars and welded them together to form a craft that he powered by muscle, using a long pole to push the boat along the sluggish water. Ava refused to get in it, and he laughed until she stomped up the bank.

They lived in a house that was not much better than a shack, but Ava's momma had given her a good kerosene lantern, so they had light. It may have not been just what she expected, but while she did carp and nag—it was her prerogative to carp and nag—she stayed.

The people were almost as wild as the country, and their language alone could knock a regular God-fearing person flat on their back. It was not that they did not believe in the Bible. It was that they believed in other things, too.

Here, when people got sick, they sent for healers—women who had a power in them that no one questioned if they were smart—and a healing woman named Lula was known to have taken a cancer out of a man named James Couch, but was called too late to save Pine Knot Johnson.

No one had to worry about the future. The old women knew how to tell it. They would dump the grounds from their coffee cups in a saucer and move it around with their fingers, and they could tell your fortune that way.

It could be something of as great import as life or death, or they might look at you and say you were going to get a letter. They read palms, and used herbs to ease morning sickness and cure a baby's croup.

People knew that if you dropped a fork, company was coming, and if a piece of food fell to the floor, it meant you secretly grudged sharing your meal.

If a snapping turtle bit you, even if you cut off its head, it would not turn loose until it thundered. Night birds were bad luck, and babies born at night were at peril if the night birds called.

And there was no ailment on earth, from a bee sting to a bullet wound, that could not be eased by daubing on a little wet snuff.

Ava listened to it all, mixing it in her mind with the doctrine of her Holiness upbringing, and stored it away. To her, the girl who loved learning, this was just a whole new kind of knowledge.

Whiskey ran through the place just as surely as the river, and on every bend, it seemed, the thin, dark trickle of smoke marked the spot of a still. Ava's man, still a boy, really, brought home money on Friday and only drank homemade likker, and on weekends they went to Newt's and wound up the Victrola, and danced on the porch.

In the week she did stoop labor, picking cotton or corn, tended her own garden and waited for a child.

And late at night, after supper, she read him the newspaper. He sat beside her, and she would have taught him to read if he had wanted, but they never got around to it. He could sign his name, and he could do math—because a boss man would cheat a worker who could not count—but to him books were a secret, locked up tight. And no one wanted a hammer swinger who quoted poetry.

And so they lived. He was different from many men of his time and place. If they were in the same general area, they sat or stood together. If she hung clothes, he stood at the line. And, unheard of for a man, he helped her cook. She made the biscuits and he fried the meat—steak when he had just finished a job, or pork chops, or thick smoked bacon—and made the gravy. There was plenty of work then, so they ate good, real good. There were no one-egg days, but two- and three-egg days. They lived, though simply, richly, if rich means a good cup of coffee.

They did not have a car, but had a mule who hated most human beings, for reasons that only mules can tell. The mule would pull a plow if he wanted, but he often did not want to plow in a straight line. When anyone put him in harness, he would start out in a clean, straight line down the row and then just turn hard right or left and, as fast as he could, snort and buck and drag the plow and the cussing plowboy across the field. He would also lie down and refuse to get up, even when Charlie demanded it—and he always seemed to hate Charlie a little less than most.

Finally Charlie learned that if he went in the house and got his shotgun and sent one shot high across the mule's ears—kind of like firing a warning shot across a ship's bow—the mule would snort indignantly, bray at the sky and rise.

If he and Ava had to go a good ways off, to town or to family, he saddled the mule and she climbed up, cautiously, behind her husband, arms locked around his waist, and they traveled. If that mule bucked, he would club it one good time across the ears, which sounds a tad mean but not to anyone who has ever had to argue with a mule. And Ava would mumble to his back about why in God's name did they not own a wagon.

He was good to her, except for calling her "Four-Eyes," and he was never mean to her when he drank. In fact, she never saw him drink. She just dealt with the fallout.

Once every few months he would not come home for supper, and it was torture for a wife still not eighteen. But late at night she would hear a slow thud of hoofbeats in the yard, and she would carry her good lantern out to the porch, to see Charlie's mule stomping into the yard.

Charlie would be drunk as Cooter Brown and singing cowboy music, and if he had not lost his hat, he waved it, and tried to get the mule to rear up like he was Tom Mix or Lash LaRue.

But mules rear from the back end, and the mule—it was such a distasteful creature that it was never given a name—would fling its hind legs straight out and duck its head and Charlie would go flying to the earth headfirst, too drunk to alter his trajectory.

The mule, to his credit, would not stomp him to death, and would step carefully around Charlie—a good mule will do that—and trot to the pasture. And Ava, depending on how mad she was at him, would sit her lantern on the porch and go down and half carry, half drag him up to his bed.

Or not. And he would lay on the ground, mumbling about how, someday, Lord, he sure would like to have him a nice, gentle horse, one that would let him down easy. After a while he would notice that he was alone, that the ground was hard and that the night was cold, and go hunt for a door handle that—dammit to hell—didn't seem to be where he had left it. He must have wasted years, groping for that knob.

\* \* \*

Her tongue was sharp, from the beginning. And, in the beginning, he liked it that way.

She was more prone to voice her opinion, probably, than most women of that time, and with Ava there was never any such thing as a compromise. But while she complained a lifetime about being cast into the damned wilderness, she always knew she had found something in this man that she had never seen in another, certainly not in any of the Congregational Holiness she had known since birth.

He talked to her.

He did not grunt about crops and scripture. He talked.

If he dug a well, he did not say, "Well, today I dug a well."

It might just be a hole in the ground, but he made it seem like a tunnel into adventure.

"You should have been there, Ava," he told her once as they sat at their little table, their heads close together within the circle of lamplight.

"Why would I want to be in the bottom of a damn hole," said Ava, who cussed more than most Congregational Holiness in that place and time.

"Because of the Chinaman," he said.

"What?" she said.

"The Chinaman," he said.

"A Chinaman helped you dig that well?"

"Naw. I met one, in the middle, a'comin' the other way."

She just looked at him, her eyes glittering behind her wire-rimmed spectacles.

"It was a deep well," he said. And as much as she hated to, she laughed at him, and laughed with him, and then told him he was pitiful, surely. "All you study," she said to him, "is folly."

But it beat the hell out of talking about cotton.

He kidded her, and egged on her natural cussedness, and he would look oh-so-wounded when she let him have it.

"Ava, Ava, Ava," he would say, shaking his head in mock dismay as she dog-cussed him in his own house. And then he just could not pretend anymore and tears would run down his face, from holding his laughter in.

It bothered her, a lot, that he was almost as good a cook as her, and that when it came to that staple of the Southern table—gravy—he had her beat. Gravy is not hard to make, but good gravy is.

When they had steak, he would stir the flour into the hot grease until it was the perfect shade of tan, and salt it just a bit—beef drippings, unlike pork, are not salty enough for a good taste—and then shake in a heavy dose of black pepper. He would stir water or milk into the roux until it was the texture of heavy cream, and they would sit down to biscuits and steak and gravy and—if it was the summer—sliced red tomatoes or cantaloupe.

And he would eat with such relish that it would make her smile, at first.

"I love steak," he would say, and if she had cooked it her eyes would light up.

"But God," he would say, "ain't the gravy good."

She would dog-cuss him some more.

"Ava, Ava, Ava."

* * *

Her education continued. She learned that you never scrub an iron skillet too hard, and you have to season it, with a little bacon grease and a rag, before you hang it on the nail for the coming morning.

She learned that, if the paycheck was lean, a few chicken gizzards fried crisp were just as good as steak, if the bicuits were good.

One day they were at the table and he noticed a difference in her, more in her face than anything else, like a shadow of nothing.

"What you worried about, Four-Eyes," he asked her, and she put his hand on her stomach. And in that instant, that tiny instant, the boy she laughed with became something else, something better. And, in a way, she did, too.

"Momma, Momma, Momma," he said.

He would never call her anything else.

# 7.

# Dead dogs and rolling steel

*Outside Rome, and in the Gadsden mills*

1925–1929

The midwife's name was Granny Isom, and she looked like she was a hundred, and might have been. She was about the size of a nine-year-old, a gnarled, skinny, short-tempered little woman, and if you had smoothed out the wrinkles she probably would have just disappeared. But for the people in Floyd County, Georgia, people too poor or too far out or just too damn hardheaded to use a town doctor, she was an angel, and countless babies passed through her hands.

Granny Isom did not think much of the miracle of birth, perhaps because it was such a common thing, and she did not suffer meddling and nervous daddies or wailing women in the little houses and the riverside shacks where she practiced something very close to medicine.

"Git out!" was the way she greeted men at their own door.

She did not say anything to the children, who ran like hell at the sight of her.

\* \* \*

She came to Ava for the first time on March 2, 1925.

Ava was big as a barn with her first baby, and told Charlie that she thought it was about time—that, or the sweet Lord was just taking her home, because what else could hurt so terrible bad. Charlie saddled his mule and rode it half to death to fetch the old midwife while Ava waited in a tiny frame house deep in the woods near Curryville, in northwest Georgia. She was seventeen.

They made it back in plenty of time. Ava, who never did one thing quietly, screamed and yelled and cussed, almost certainly, as the miracle unfolded. When it was over, the midwife handed her a son.

They named him James, for Charlie's daddy. In the South, you do not have to love someone a real whole lot to name a child for them. It is just something you do, naming the first boy after his grandfather.

Granny Isom did not stay long after that. What happened after that, she figured, wasn't really her fault.

We do not know what James cost. Like other professional people, she took whatever the man could afford in trade for the child— corn, a quilt, some onions, or just a pone of cornbread and some apple butter—and climbed up on a wagon seat. An angel should not have needed a mule to get home, but a short-tempered one does, I suppose.

The baby was long—male babies always run long in the family—and even in his first day on this earth he had a fine set of ears on him. His hair was sandy, like his daddy's. In fact, as the year crept by, as he looked less and less like a pink monkey and more like a human, as babies naturally do, he looked more and more like his daddy. In time it would be uncanny, how much he mirrored him, in his face, those gigantic hands, all of it.

Charlie was still just a boy himself, but if he ever was good at one thing on this earth, it was being a daddy. At that time, when he was eighteen, he knew the one thing a man needed to know.

Don't let nothin' happen to it. Kill if you have to, but don't never, ever let nothin' happen to it, because it is weak, and small, and it belongs to you. One day, twenty years later, he would seize James by the arms and say those very words to him after he had married and had a child of his own. That is how we know the code he lived by.

\* \* \*

Just a little more than a year later, on June 19 of 1926, he sent for Granny Isom again. This one they named William, also after kin, and this one, too, was long, and sprouted up tall and big-eared like his daddy. It was good that the two sons came so close together like that, because it is almost certain that one would have killed the other one if he had had any real advantage in size. By the time the boys were toddlers, just as soon as they could make a good fist, they fought— hair-pulling, eye-gouging and biting, drawing blood and raising welts and purple bruises. Charlie, Ava and other kin stripped all the low limbs off the hickory trees trying to find enough switches to discipline their boys, but it was just plain useless. The two boys considered a good beating to be more or less fair payment for the pleasure of hitting each other with rocks, pushing each other into mud holes or cow flop.

But while it was acceptable for brothers and cousins to beat you senseless, outsiders could not lay a hand on you in anger, and could not hurt you for sport, not without feeling Charlie's terrible wrath.

William saw it for the first time when he was still less than waist-high. Almost seventy years later, it makes him proud.

\* \* \*

Life in the foothills had not softened much since Charlie's childhood. Cars and trucks were creeping along the rutted roads, but men still rode mules through the streets of Rome, the county seat, still fought duels with pistols and flick-knives and even ax handles, still beat each other bloody.

The cockfights drew a hundred on a Saturday, and men whose finer dispositions had been dulled by the hard work and likker found something in the life-and-death struggle of the chicken fights that sliced through, that penetrated, that pleased. The chicken-fighters sawed the bone-hard natural spurs off the gamecocks and strapped on razor-sharp steel spurs, called gaffs, and tossed them into a pit, winner take all. The loser was served the next day with biscuits and white gravy.

But it was the dog pits that really got a man's blood up. Harsh old men with a brittle, horny place where a heart should have been took puppies and taught them to kill with kittens, and when the dogs matured the dogfighters trimmed back their ears and cut off their tails, so the other dog could not get a solid grip. They crossbred the slow and dull-witted bulldogs with leaner, faster breeds, and came up with a killer.

A man named Dempsey, who lived not far from where the Bundrums lived in Curryville, had a dog like that. He kept it in his barn, and it was mean—so mean he kept it tied with a heavy logging chain.

Ava and her boys were visiting one day and William wandered down to the barn. Old Man Dempsey thought he would have some sport as the big dog growled and pulled at his chain at the sight of the boy.

Dempsey reached down and picked up a cornstalk that was laying on the ground, and handed it to William. Then he unhooked the dog's chain from the barn wall and held it, like a leash.

"Draw that cornstalk back, boy," he said, "and make like you're gonna hit him."

William, being little, did as he was told.

He drew back the stalk and, pretend-like, swatted at the air in front of the growling, snapping dog.

Then Dempsey let go of the chain.

The dog leapt on William, snapping, and sank his teeth deep into the boy's side. The blood spurted and Old Man Dempsey, seeing that his joke had gone much too far, dragged his dog away.

But not before William's side was bit bloody. He ran hard to his momma, screaming, and if she could have found a gun or even a good stick, she would have killed Dempsey. But she just took her crying boy home, and waited for her husband to get in from work.

He came in from the job, grimed with sweat and sawdust, and listened as Ava, crying, told him what had happened.

Charlie, in anger, was the opposite of most men. While most men got mad and loud, he got quiet, so quiet, and dropped his voice so low that you had to lean in close to him to hear what he was saying.

He was deathly quiet now.

William lay in the bed, his side covered in salve—they would have put salve on a brain tumor—and bound up with clean rags.

"Son," Charlie said softly, "he eat you up pretty good, didn't he?"

"Yes sir, I believe he did," William said.

"Can you move?" his daddy said. "Can you walk?"

"Yes sir, I believe I can."

"Then let's go."

Charlie reached and got his shotgun and slung it over his shoulder. Ava stood at the door, quiet for once, and watched them go.

They got in an old cut-down truck that Charlie had bought and drove to the Dempseys'. They held hands as they walked up to the pine porch, and Charlie rapped on the front door with the gun barrel.

Old Man Dempsey cracked the door and looked out.

"What you doin' here, Bundrum, with that gun," he said.

"I've come for the dog," Charlie said softly.

"You can't have him," Dempsey said.

"I've come for the dog," Charlie said again, this time almost in a whisper, "or I've come for you."

Dempsey looked at Charlie's face.

"The dog's in the barn," he said.

Charlie walked to the barn with William at his side, and told him to wait outside. He walked in and, immediately, there was one shot. Then Charlie walked out, his face blank.

All his life, Charlie knew he should have shot the man, truly, but in Floyd County, in the 1920s, they didn't put a white man into prison, usually, for shooting a dog.

But they would strap you down and make you ride the lightning for killing a man, and who would have fed his family, if he was so foolish.

He looked down at his son.

"Let's go home, Shorty," he said.

\* \* \*

It was a hopeful time. World War I was done and the veterans had come home to sit on the courthouse benches, some trailing an empty pants leg, and tell stories of the hand-to-hand fighting in the Argonne Forest, of the choking hell of the trenches as the mustard gas poured in and the bodies stank on the barbed wire in no-man's-land. But this was peacetime and there was good work in the steel mills and pipe shops in Gadsden and Anniston over in Alabama, and in the textile mills on the Georgia side.

Charlie wore a carpenter's apron and built homes for the soldiers who came home, then landed a good job, for real money, at the steel plant in Gadsden, an industrial town alongside the Coosa. His brother-in-law, Tobe Morrison, helped him get on.

He rolled steel, working in heat that burned the hairs off his arms, beating at sparks that singed his hair and his eyebrows and made his lungs prickle. He shoveled coal into the coke ovens where the heat would melt your shoes and make you faint, and loaded box-cars with new, fresh steel, so new it didn't even have any rust on it. And on payday, when the smut-covered men lined up for their money—the gentry there called them "smoke necks"—he laughed and laughed.

Gadsden was like a lot of industrial cities in the South, a city that went from nothing to something really fast. The workers, some who had been behind a mule just the week before, built little frame houses with real porches, and sometimes the company even built them for their workers. It was a different time, then, when companies did things like that. If a man wasn't afraid to work, he could have things he never dreamed of.

Charlie bought a new car, a 1928 Whippet, and they rented a house in Attalla, near Gadsden, which was almost close enough to the country to suit him—he could not rest, he always said, in town.

He and Ava bought some nice clothes from the Sears and Roebuck and had their pictures made, and Ava started buying pocketbooks—she loved pocketbooks.

While they were in Attalla, living fat and easy at the corner of First and Forest, Ava gave Charlie a daughter. A genuine doctor—with plaques on the wall and a necktie—delivered the baby girl.

Edna was born on September 3, 1929, and as proud as he was about his sons, Edna tickled him to death. Even when she was small, he propped her on his shoulders and took her with him when he went fishing. She had brown hair, and even as a toddler she was unusually brave, and not a bit squeamish about fishworms or catfish or other slime-covered things. She was tough, which was good. Otherwise her brothers might have killed her, probably by accident but not necessarily so.

"He would take me places and not take James and William," Edna said, proud of the time they stole.

Edna would be the model older sister, old beyond her years,

and a strong right hand to Ava. She snapped beans, sewed, and as other babies came, she helped look after them. Edna was the glue. As Ava ranted, Edna soothed. As Ava fumed, Edna looked for solutions. Even as a little girl, Edna would sometimes seem older than her momma, sewing clothes for the younger children and helping to cook. But as a baby, before there was work to do, she rode her daddy's bony shoulders to the creek, and laughed and clapped her hands when he pulled in a fish.

Some men love daughters more. Charlie was just one of them.

* * *

It was a good family, or at least a good start on one, and a good life. A man could afford things. He could feed his children hot biscuits, ham and fresh cantaloupe on Sunday, and buy his oranges by the bushel. His wife didn't have to count the eggs and make water gravy, because milk was not such a precious thing that you had to meter it out by the ounce. Ava, used to this life, this abundance, was not impressed much, but Charlie, a poor boy all his life, went a little wild. He bought a slouch hat, like a movie star would wear, and had his first taste of store-bought likker. He thought it was bland. Like many things, if it's legal, it cannot be all that good. But he liked that hat, and went all the way to Anniston—one whole county away—to have his picture made on Noble Street.

It would last forever, that life, because steel would have to roll forever. It had to. How could you build a country without steel?

Ava, who hated the deep woods, loved living in a place where the stores were right there, right there in front of her, and a person could sit on their front porch at night and see a light—a real electric one—glowing just a few feet away in the window of a neighbor's house. Here you could walk to church, or take your babies to the doctor. In the cool of the evenings people would walk past the porch and say, "How do?" And, best of all, there was the money—never enough to pile up too high but enough to pay their way, to buy groceries and pay rent, so that a person did not have to be ashamed at the first of the month.

And if a child got sick, Ava opened her pocketbook and bought the medicine it took to make them well again or paid the doctor to heal them, which is how life is supposed to be. How could it ever be any other way?

Who would ever let such a thing happen.

\* \* \*

The plant laid him off not long after Edna's second birthday, but it wasn't personal. U.S. Steel had 225,000 full-time employees in 1929—and zero four years later. It had changed the lives of a whole generation of Southerners who found that rolling steel was child's play next to what they had done, next to cutting pulpwood or fighting a brain-dead beast along endless rows of red dirt. And now, it was changing them back.

People would come to call it the Great Depression.

For Ava and Charlie, it was as if the biggest broom in the world just dropped out of the sky and swept everything away. Charlie could do a whole lot more besides work in the steel mill, he could make a living. But he could not make that living, he could not give them that life.

Town cost too much. They went back to the woods.

# 8.

## Little Hoover

*Curryville, Georgia*

Edna stood beside the bed, amazed, and just watched her. She did not know a person could be so small. Her momma told her she would get bigger with time, and that was true, for a while.

They had come back to Georgia to live, where Charlie could always jerk a living from the hills and the river around Curryville, if he had a little luck on his trotline or in the woods with his .410. Now there was a new child to feed, but instead of worrying he stepped lighter, taller.

The baby had jet-black hair, like her mother. Charlie called her "Little Hoover," a dark joke in honor of a failed president who watched, helplessly, as his own federal soldiers attacked and destroyed a raggedy squatters' village of homeless, destitute World War I veterans who asked for early payment of their pensions. Douglas MacArthur and George Patton, not yet heroes, cleansed the capital of the poor, and that news, carried down to the South in faded, secondhand newspapers, made common men like Charlie Bundrum despise the remote politician and gentlemen soldiers.

The baby's real name was Emma Mae. Born on May 29, 1931, she entered the world in a black time.

For Edna, then just old enough to understand the struggle between life and death, the year is carved deep, deep in her mind.

"I watched her sleep on the bed when Momma was out picking some onions, and she woke up and squirmed around and fell behind that bed. I just started crying, 'I can't get her, I can't get her.' Momma came in, threw a bunch of onions down and got her and held on to her. 'To hell with them onions,' she said."

Edna hoped the baby would get big enough so she couldn't fall behind the bed again. But in spring, she started getting smaller.

"She had the diarrhea real bad. They boiled milk and boiled water. Momma nursed her by laying her on a pillow 'cause she was so little. Then she took the pneumonia, real bad."

A hospital could have saved her. Medicine could have helped. Edna does not remember ever going to a hospital or seeing any medicine in the house, but then she was just a child herself. She just remembers that she and her brothers James and William ate cornbread then—just cornbread.

"She was buried not long before sundown, not far from a holly tree. I stood on a hill and watched Momma and Daddy stand there at the grave, and I didn't have on no coat or shoes and the wind was cold on my legs. And I watched the sun go down and they was still standing there."

There was no money for a real headstone. But before he left the graveyard, Charlie gathered white chert rocks from the hillside and laid them on the grave, being very careful about it, as if painting some kind of design with them on the ground. Edna did not understand why he did it, but as he worked Ava stood by him and watched, paying attention.

Then he took her arm and they walked off the hill together.

Edna understood little of it, really, just that they left Emma Mae at Curryville when they moved not long after that, and that her daddy, who always laughed even when he hit his thumb with a hammer, who would grab up his children, pop them down on his bony shoulders and walk for miles, seemed to sleepwalk through the weeks. Edna, puzzled, wondered why he was quiet, because he was never that quiet. He even stopped singing. To Edna, it seemed like some strange new man lived in her daddy's old clothes, a man who didn't know the words.

"The one thing," she said, "that whupped my daddy."

Something seemed to go out of Ava, too. "I always figured Momma didn't like me anymore because of Emma Mae and what happened," but that was how a child would have taken it, the coldness that enveloped Ava in that time.

It might have been better if she had stayed in the mountains of Curryville for a while, where she could sit under a holly tree and pick weeds off a tiny grave, the way people do. It shouldn't have cost nothin', really, just to be still awhile.

# 9.

# Movers

---

## *The foothills*

Ava hated moving day. When everything was loaded and tied down, she sat red-eyed and tight-lipped in the passenger seat of the Model A, her hands wrapped not around one of her babies but around something almost as dear, her kerosene lamp. Her husband could not abide living poor in town, so he usually rented houses at the lost end of a dirt road, deep in the pine barrens and old-growth hardwood forests, surrounded by poison ivy and blackberry bushes as impenetrable as trench wire. The power lines seldom reached so far, and the nighttime came alive with wild things, hidden things. No matter how many times you tell yourself a screech owl is just a bird, when you hear it in the dark woods, it sounds like murder in the trees. Ava's lamp, made of glass as thick as a Coke bottle, was her island, a circle of safe, amber light. Candles, no matter how many you light, are too flimsy for the woods. Ava knew that a ghost would walk right on past a candle and say hello.

Electricity might have caught up with them if they had stayed in one place long enough, but there was no profit in sitting still. Charlie, smelling like heat and tar from the shingles he pounded into place, would come in the house and tell Ava that the job had dried up, but that he had heard there was work over in Alabama, or over in Georgia. It happened at least once a year, often twice, sometimes three times a year.

In the decade of the Depression, they moved twenty-one times.

The prosperity they would chase, crisscrossing the state line in that overloaded, rattletrap, cut-down Ford, was usually only marginally better than the life they had left behind. The ladders he climbed, in the summer heat that turned the shingles to black mush, in the cold that made them crack like panes of glass, never got him more than a few feet higher than rock bottom, and the wells he dug were just dead-end tunnels leading to a wadded-up ten-dollar bill. Maybe prosperity is too strong a word for it. They pursued the here and now, a sack of flour, a gallon of kerosene, a yard of copper tubing, a new needle and thread.

They would have loved him anyway, if times had not been so hard, if he had not saved them from it, but would they have loved him as much? It is easy to be liked when the world has no jagged edges, when life is electric blankets and peach ice cream. But to be beloved, a man needs a dragon.

History gave him one.

The stock market crash of October 24, 1929, Black Thursday, wafted down into the Deep South like a slow-working disease. Even now, seventy years later, old people still thank God that they lived in the country, where the shame of their poverty was hidden by the trees.

It was a creeping thing, down here, not the drama that sent the Yankee stockbrokers leaping from window ledges. In a part of the nation still wasted from Reconstruction, this "Great Depression" was, at first, almost redundant, like putting the bootheels to a man already down. It did not make the rows any longer for a farmer plowing a mule, or change the diet of a family already eating cornbread and beans seven days a week. It took a while to feel it. But in time, it even found the people at the ends of the dirt roads.

It is true that almost everyone in the foothills farmed and hunted, so there were no breadlines, no men holding signs that begged for work and food, no children going door to door, as they did in Atlanta, asking for table scraps. Here, deep in the woods, was a different agony. Babies, the most tenuous, died from poor diet and simple things, like fevers and dehydration. In Georgia, one in seven babies died before their first birthday, and in Alabama it was worse.

You could feed your family catfish and jack salmon, poke salad and possum, but medicine took cash money, and the poorest of the poor, blacks and whites, did not have it. Women, black and white, really did smother their babies to save them from slow death, to give a stronger, sounder child a little more, and stories of it swirled round and round until it became myth, because who can live with that much truth.

People did go hungry. Meanwhile, on the lawn of the White House, President Hoover was photographed feeding his dog.

\* \* \*

They were living north of Rome when Juanita came—again, with Granny Isom's grim-faced supervision—on April 22, 1934. Her full name is Gracie Juanita, which is about as grand a name as I ever heard, as if Charlie and Ava were fighting back against the stinginess of the years with that forty-dollar name. But the baby was small and slight, and her momma and daddy were afraid for her. Emma Mae was fresh on their minds.

She would get sick, and Ava died a little every time. Her mind was not built for worry, for being sad. It could not absorb it somehow, the way some ground can't hold water. She prayed hard, her eyes closed. She prayed a lot. Charlie would stand over the bed, helpless. He could have gotten down on his knees, too, but he was not a praying man, then. It could be that he did talk to God, but inside his own mind, standing up, the way some proud men insist on doing it. But I guess we'll never know that either.

All around them babies had slipped away, but Juanita thrived in time. Juanita grew up fine. She was not sickly, just bony, and she would be bony all her life. She was just uninterested in food, and eating was something she endured.

The girl they just called "Niter" inherited her daddy's hands—not the size, but the skill in them—and made playhouses from branches and scraps when she was just a toddler, building things and tearing them down and building them again. Some girls wanted dolls. She wanted a good hammer.

Once, when she was still small, Edna built herself a playhouse out of tree branches and refused to let Juanita play in it. Nita just stood looking at it a moment, figuring, then built one just like it.

Then Edna's mysteriously caught on fire.

"I helped her put it out, after a while," Juanita recalls.

*　*　*

His children say, today, that they never really noticed the pain and the poverty that swirled around them, because he loomed over it and would never let it reach them. They did not mind that they ate a whole lot of cornbread, did not notice—not until much later—that Charlie and Ava waited to eat until the children had, to make sure there was enough.

Outside their protection, outside that perimeter of pride and love, the long, bad years writhed on, coiling and coiling upon themselves like a snake they couldn't kill.

Ragged tent cities took shape beside lonely Southern blacktop, on riverbanks, beside railroad tracks. By the early 1930s, one in three men in the foothills was out of work. Cotton farms failed because the textile mills were padlocked, and cotton rotted in the dirt.

In the mills that survived, the owners slashed wages in half, by seventy-five percent and even more. Hard men who would have half killed another man for even the vaguest insult just bowed their heads to it, to survive.

It was bad here but at least it was a little warmer, and county sheriffs armed with ax handles waited at railroad depots and at lonely crossroads to discourage the out-of-work men who came south looking for work or just a more pleasant place to wait it all out.

Aristocratic Southerners, the ones who somehow held on to the old money that set them above and apart, did not, history shows, do a lot for their brethren. And some even seemed to take sadistic pleasure in driving poorer Southerners, a class they had long disdained, to even greater pain.

"Let 'em starve," said Eugene Talmadge, a Depression-era governor of Georgia who refused to aid federal efforts to give destitute people of his own state a pittance to help them survive, who stalled, harassed and demanded the names of every person receiving federal aid.

In hell, as Ava used to say, there is a special box seat reserved for all those bow-tie-wearing, imperious sons of bitches.

In Alabama and Georgia, people wore out their last good suit of clothes and just stopped going to church because they were ashamed, and preachers nailed signs to fence posts to remind their flocks that old, faded dresses and ragged overalls were not offensive in the eyes of the Lord. Here, eight out of ten schoolchildren stopped coming because the books and teachers cost money, and even now old women will tell you one of the most hateful things about the Depression was that it stole books, teachers and knowledge, and held another generation prisoner to the old life of backbreaking work, a life in which every book may as well have had a chain wrapped around it, for all the good it did a person who did not read.

People with deep roots stood fast in the doorways of ancestral homes, and lost everything. People without roots, the wanderers like Charlie Bundrum, drifted with the times, and survived.

\* \* \*

He could do sawmill work, build houses and barns, pound shingles, strip cane, plow a mule, lay brick, do stoop labor and, if the law would just leave him alone, run off a little shine. But he had to keep moving, going to the work, so he would wander, dragging Ava and a varying number of children with him, first in a mule-drawn wagon, then in his truck. It was a car, really, but he had used a torch to hack off the back part and then rigged a flat wooden bed on it, because you can't haul anything but relatives in a backseat. On moving day he piled it high with mattresses, rocking chairs, chickens, girls, boys and, her daughters recall, "about ninety pocketbooks." Ava didn't have anything much to put inside one, but she had, in truth, dozens of cheap, dime-store purses, which she counted on moving day to make sure she had them all. She could always come back and get a chair or a chicken and even a child, but people would steal a good pocketbook.

It usually took at least two trips. They had to come back and get the cow. If it was a short move, the children walked the cow, for miles, at the side of the road. But if it was a long one, he hoisted the heifer on the cut-down and drove away, the cow, wild-eyed and bleating, going backward at thirty-five miles an hour.

After a while, the cow would run when she saw Charlie coming at her with a halter or a rope, and for years she kicked anyone who milked her. I guess she was just getting even.

For a few dollars a month, they rented little frame houses in the hills around Gadsden and Rome, on farmland above Noccalula Falls, on Bean Flat Mountain, in Whites Gap, on the Piedmont Highway, Boozer's Lake Road, Littlejohn Road, Cove Road, and on the lovely-sounding Carpenter's Lane. Some places had no names, and are remembered only by the landlords. There was the Osby place, the Buchanan place, the Coot Green place and the Coot Stevenson place. You have to move a lot to live in two different houses owned by two different men named Coot.

Ava and the children picked cotton for some of their landlords to help pay the rent, but as the Depression wore on that work was scarce, too. Charlie was the machine that powered their lives, pushing them from place to place.

For his family, there was none of the excitement of a brand-new beginning. Birds live that way, not people. His wife and children knew, every time they pulled up in another red-dirt driveway, that it was not actually home. In a home, you notice the trees getting taller.

Home was the driveway, any driveway, that they saw their daddy walk up in the cool of the evening. It was always a new porch, but the same rocker, the same laps to crawl into, the same voice singing about patience and salvation from the open window, the same old saddle horse or mule cropping grass in the yard. And in time, everything there would be just one more memory. To this day, his girls have no trouble recounting specific stories about that time, and don't waver much as to dates and ages and most other pertinent facts. But they often have trouble as to the where of it. The where, it all runs together.

Ava cried, but cried harder if they were leaving Georgia. She had been born in Alabama and loved living in Gadsden in the fat years, and that should have been where her heart was. But if she was going to live in a damn jungle, she preferred it be a damn jungle in Georgia, she always said, and never saw any reason to elaborate on that. At least she had the comfort of knowing that she would never be very far from the Peach State—her husband never moved more than a hundred miles in any direction—and that she would be back within its borders soon enough. It was almost as if life had tied Charlie Bundrum to the end of a string and staked down the other end on the Alabama-Georgia line. He could ramble, but just so far.

It was about this time that he started a few gallons of likker, to swap for meal and bacon and coffee. Sometimes, to be accurate, they moved not in search of work but because one of the lawmen had found one of Charlie's stills. That did not mean Charlie went to jail, because finding a still, hard as that was, did not mean you had found him. The lawmen often knocked at houses that echoed from the emptiness inside, and neighbors would smile, knowing that Charlie and his cow were safe across the state line.

*　　*　　*

The presidential election of Franklin D. Roosevelt, though he was an aristocrat himself, brought work with the WPA, and thin, weak hope. People from the foothills wrote to Eleanor Roosevelt asking if she had a spare coat they could use till times got better. "Nothing fancy, please," a woman wrote. "All my clothes are plain." Another woman sent Eleanor her wedding ring as collateral for a loan, so she could buy her baby clothes. "I don't want charity," the woman wrote. Meanwhile, striking textile mill workers in Georgia were herded into makeshift, barbed-wire prisons—the equivalent of concentration camps—by lawmen armed with shotguns.

"Better Times Are on the Way," read a department-store ad in the *Atlanta Journal* after Roosevelt's inauguration. The same ad offered its readers three months' worth of toothpaste for one dollar, and said people could postdate checks three months ahead, when, surely, times down here would be better.

"I hope to believe this," wrote an out-of-work man in a letter to columnist Mildred Seydell of the *Georgian* newspaper. "How it hurts, to know you are almost starving in a land of plenty."

I wonder, sometimes, what Ava saw in the bottoms of the

coffee cups. Did she see a decade of hardship ahead, or did she have faith in this crippled rich man who used a cigarette holder but talked humanely about poor people in the pages of the week-old newspapers.

When federal aid finally did trickle into the foothills, it was a fraction of what other regions got—as if a baby in the honeysuckle did not need as much milk, as much medicine.

Ava gave up after a while, not on living, just on staying anyplace long enough to really get to know it, to see the trees get taller.

He would walk in and gently tell Ava, "Four-Eyes, we got to go," then loaded up his life on the truck bed and hauled it away, his children holding tight to dogs that did not seem to mind all the motion, as long as someone tossed them a hard biscuit every now and then. He would grind the gears and not even look back, because everything of value would be with him when he stopped again, unless he bounced someone off or one of the chickens committed suicide somewhere along Highway 9. Strangers pulled the weeds that sprouted over the one thing he could not carry with him, because even the dead were a luxury. So they rambled, and while they never really made it anyplace better, he knew how to take them there.

And Ava would be beside him, the kerosene sloshing back and forth in her beacon, her hands cradling the heavy, smut-blackened glass like it was leaded crystal. Setting up house was never hard for her.

All she had to do was find a match.

*　　*　　*

Some historians say the time that defines us, as a people, was the Civil War, and I guess that is true for those Southerners who hold tight to yellowed daguerreotypes of defiant colonels, distant ancestors who glare at the camera like it was a cannon, leaning on their swords.

But you seldom hear people of the foothills talk much about the

Civil War, contrary to the popular belief that all of us down here are sitting around waiting for the South to Rise Again, gazing at our etching of Robert E. Lee and sipping whiskey from the silver cups our great-aunt hid in the corncrib when she saw the Yankees comin'.

But you hear them talk a lot about the Depression, at reunions, at dinner on the ground, on that bench outside E. L. Green's store, down the road from my momma's house. They cannot tell you who commanded much of anything at Little Round Top or Missionary Ridge, but they know the names of all the knothead mules that dragged their daddies cussing and sweating across ground so poor that grass would not grow, and will look you dead in the eye and tell you that, yes, people really did work themselves to death. The Depression, endured in the lifetimes of people we know, was our time of heroes and martyrs, and our monuments are piled neatly on the ground.

## 10.

# Hootie

*The banks of the Oostanaula*

THE LATE 1930S

*Let's put it this way. A woman wouldn't run herself to death going after him.*

—JUANITA, ON JESSIE "HOOTIE" CLINES

On the river, among the dragons that slumbered in the deep caves along its banks and the mysterious things that called down from the dark trees, was a gremlin.

His name was Jessie Clines, but everyone just called him Hootie. He was a dusty, scrawny man, about five feet high in his bootheels, and would have weighed less than a hundred pounds if his trouser pockets had not always been filled with silver dimes—just dimes.

He had a face like a pickax. His nose was long and hooked, and pointy on the end, like he had bought it at the Dollar Store and tied it on his face with a string, and it curved all the way down past his lips. I would not have believed it if the people telling me his story had not raised their right hand to God.

He had beady eyes, set in close on his nose. And if he had one tooth in his head, it would have died of loneliness. He always smelled like woodsmoke and bait.

He could go entire days without saying a word, and when he did talk his voice was reedy and high. He always wore an old army uniform, but he had never been in the army. He just liked the suit. His britches had holes in them, many holes, and he wore red long-handle underwear, which was plain to see.

He wore a long-billed fisherman's cap, the kind the rich men wore in their yachts on salt water, and it had a leaping blue marlin stenciled on the crown. Hootie probably never saw a marlin, or saw an ocean, but he loved that hat. When it wore out—actually, when the hat just rotted off his head—he got a felt slouch hat, like the one Jimmy Cagney wore.

He wore discarded shoes, and cut holes in them if they were too tight, or just for ventilation.

"Daddy wore holes in his shoes," said Juanita. "Hootie just cut holes in his."

He lived down on the river in a tiny shack. No one seemed to know if he owned it, had once owned it or just squatted there. He had just always been there, living on fish and whiskey, trading one for the other.

His only luxury was potted meat, a paste made from ground meat, and he ate it by scooping it out of the tiny flat cans with his pinkie finger. The cans, gold-colored, were hidden around his tiny shack like Easter eggs. Inside, he cured animal skins—beaver, rat, fox, other things—and the smell was enough to knock you back out the door.

His shack teetered on a steep bank, just above the brown river, hidden completely in the summer by the thick green. It was as far back, as remote, as a man could live. Leaves rotted a foot deep on the ground and the vines and pines and hardwoods blocked the sun, and it was still and quiet and cool in the summer. If a man wanted to live alone, it was probably as good a place as any to be left that way.

They called him Hootie because he talked to the owls. The woods on the river were full of owls—they hunted the banks for rats, ground squirrels, chipmunks and just about anything else that moved—and the calls they gave really did sound like "hoot, hoot," but trembling, like what you imagined a ghost would sound like.

He could answer them, and it sounded just the same.

People would see him on the bank, working his trotline or traps, and point at him and either laugh or stare. But Hootie only looked like a gremlin. He was too harmless for that, too good-natured. He was more like an elf.

He wasn't even a real hermit. Hermits do not get lonely. Hootie had.

Charlie first saw Hootie when he was fishing the river near his shack. He waved at the little man.

Hootie just stood there.

Charlie waved again.

Hootie stuck his hand up in the air, as if surprised that it didn't hurt. Charlie walked up the riverbank and Hootie stood there, acting like he wanted to run. Charlie looked him up and down.

"Well," Charlie said, "you shore ain't purty, are you, son?"

Hootie shook his head.

"I've got some biscuit, if you want some?"

Hootie nodded, hard.

Friendships get started on less than that.

To Charlie he was not a gnome or an outcast, just another person to tell tales to, to catch fish with, another man who preferred campfire to the glare of electric light.

From that moment, Hootie followed him around like a new puppy. Charlie, who could talk enough for any two men, did not mind the fact that Hootie just smiled, listening, and was not prone to interrupt.

He was not retarded, just quiet and a little bit slow, but people thought he wasn't right because he would not always answer them when they spoke to him. He was just shy, achingly shy. Life had probably made him that way, made him live in his own head.

He could never have lived in town. There were a lot of men on the river then who couldn't have. Charlie was almost one of them, but it was just too lonely on the river for a man who wanted friends, a wife, and an ever-growing number of babies crawling round him on the floor.

So, instead of being a place he lived in, it was a place he went to, to get away from life for a while, and Hootie was always there.

The two men, one so tall, one so small, built fires and passed a mason jar of hooch back and forth, and cooked fish over the fire on thin pieces of steel that Hootie had scavenged from a junkyard, or in an old iron skillet that Charlie carried in a tow sack with his hooks and line. With the help of Charlie's sons, they dug mussels from the sandbars and used them to bait their lines, and snatched the giant cats from the eddies. And through it all Charlie talked.

"I like to hear you talk, Mr. Charlie," Hootie said once, out of the blue.

"Well, son," Charlie said, "we are both fortunate."

Charlie always called him son, even though Hootie was probably twenty years older than him. Somehow, it just seemed right.

It went on that way for about a year. Charlie saw him every month or so, always on the river.

Some people would have said he was mysterious, which is just a fancy way of saying he was lied about. There were more lies told about Jessie "Hootie" Clines than any man on the river, and it almost killed him.

\* \* \*

In time, as word of the little hermit's presence leaked out, the stories came.

Some people said Hootie was a wounded hero from the Great War who had been horribly mutilated—that would explain his appearance, because nobody is born that ugly—and others said he was a circus performer who had committed some terrible crime under the big top. That, or he fell off the circus train as it passed through north Georgia. Some said he had escaped from a loony house.

And some said he had robbed a bank up north—in Chicago, maybe, or Indiana—and that all the other members of his gang had been gunned down. Hootie, they said, had escaped with thousands in silver dollars.

They said he came here to this isolated place to lay low—no one seemed to mind that he had been laying low for thirty years—and that he had hidden the money on the river.

Some people even said he had buried the money all around his yard in mason jars, and that he dug it up every now and then, to feel it in his hands.

If the stories had been true, Jessie Clines would have been the most famous man on the state line. Instead, there was just enough rumor, enough myth, to draw people to him, and many of them were bad.

The river was still a lawless place then. One night a group of men came to Hootie's shack and told him they wanted his money, and they commenced to beat him. They passed a bottle and beat him, for a long, long time.

It became a ritual. Every now and then, a group of drunks would catch him in his bed, and make a game out of it. Some people are just a waste of human skin, and these people were that kind.

Sometimes they just beat him a little, slapping his jaws back and forth, and sometimes they beat him pretty bad, putting their boots to him—there is no mistaking a mark from a bootheel. No one knows why he did not pack his few pitiful belongings and run. It may be he had no place to go, or that even this was better than how he had lived before he drifted here.

One day Charlie came and he saw what the river trash had done to Hootie. Both his eyes were blacked, his lips were split and he was still bleeding from his mouth. When Charlie asked Hootie who had beaten him so badly, Hootie refused to answer.

Charlie sat with him all day, and that night he laid Hootie down on his cot—all Hootie ever slept on was an old army cot—and walked down to his car to fetch his roofing hatchet.

He waited on the stoop of the shack all night, his hatchet in his right hand, hoping. But no one came.

The next morning, he told Hootie to pack up his clothes and come with him.

"You can't stay here, and I got to work and can't stay with you," he told Hootie.

He took him home to their little place in the country, outside Rome.

"What you doin' with him?" Ava asked when she saw Hootie sitting on the porch.

"He's gonna stay with us for a while," Charlie said, and he explained what had happened, how the river trash had abused him.

"We barely got enough for us," Ava said.

"We'll have enough," Charlie said.

Ava, who considered it a point of pride that she would go to her grave without ever letting anyone have the last word on anything, said she reckoned it would be fine, for a while.

It would be years before Charlie found out who had beaten his friend, and the anger should have cooled by then. It should have.

\* \* \*

He slept on a pallet on the floor, or on a cot, or outside, when he needed to be by himself. He almost never spoke, but he would sit with Charlie and Ava's children on the porch as the talk swirled around him.

He smoked hand-rolled cigarettes, and when he was done with the tiny cloth pouches, he gave them to the girls. They put them on sticks and made a doll.

And sometimes, when they were sick, or just because he felt like it, he would give them dimes. They jingled in his pockets when he walked and he never seemed to run out, as if there really was some magic in the little man.

The only things he owned in the world, he kept in a tiny bundle, the kind hoboes used to carry when they hopped trains. He had a spare shirt and a spare pair of pants—old army clothes, too.

"And," Juanita said, "he slept in his hat."

No one bothered him for a long time because he was almost always within the tall man's orbit, and the trash who had hurt him apparently figured it was just not worth the pain.

\* \* \*

About a year after Charlie adopted him, the work dried up there in north Georgia. Charlie and Ava packed up the children and belongings for a move to Alabama, and waited, the car's engine running, for Hootie to climb on board.

Charlie blew the horn and motioned for him, but Hootie just stood there.

He had left his shack on the river, where he had been for as long as anyone could remember, and now Charlie wanted to take him even farther away. It must have seemed like the cut-down was a rocket ship to the moon.

"I need you to make sure the kids don't fall out," Charlie said. Hootie's job was, indeed, to stretch his legs across the tailgate of the truck—he was shaped funny and had long legs for a little man—and he took that job seriously.

But this time he just stood there, his chin—well, if he had a chin—tucked on his breast.

Finally Charlie put the truck in gear and rolled away, leaving Hootie standing in the yard.

＊　＊　＊

In Alabama, they unloaded the truck and unpacked, and Ava cooked supper. Charlie stood on the porch, lost in thought. Then he walked back to his truck, slammed the door so hard that it boomed, and sped off down the dirt road, heading east.

He found Hootie sitting on the steps of the empty house.

Hootie hopped in the front seat.

They went home.

＊　＊　＊

Hootie helped Charlie work sometimes, for decent wages. He ate at their table, and was treated like family. "I never remember when he wasn't there," Juanita said.

Sometimes their friends would ask them who the funny-looking little man was, and they always said the same thing: "That's Hootie. Daddy got him off the river."

"Why?" the other children always said.

# 11.

# The big end

*Northeastern Alabama*

AS THE DEPRESSION DEEPENED

Times was hard enough, Ava felt, without having to deal with the morons.

People still talk of the night the three drunk men kicked at the door in the middle of the night, shouting for him to come and drink some shine. One of the men was named Martin and everybody knew he didn't have the brains God gave a water bug. With his babies in bed, Charlie had too much good sense to let such men in his home, even in daylight.

"Y'all git," he said, loud, so his voice would carry through the pine. "These babies is sleepin'."

"Come on, Bundrum. We got a quart," growled Martin from the other side of the door. A whole country in need of food, but the clear whiskey still ran like water.

Before Charlie could swing his legs out of bed, all three men started hammering on the door.

"I said git," Charlie shouted, and reached for his overalls. Ava sat bolt upright but still, a hurricane forming on her features, and the children looked from the door to their daddy, big-eyed.

"Let us in, Chollie," said Martin, his voice slurred, "or I'll kick it in." One man giggled as another, apparently Martin, kicked one, two, three times at the door, and then they all started kicking until the door trembled on its hinges.

Charlie's tool belt was inside, and he reached down and drew his hammer—about a pound of good iron on the end of an oak handle—from its loop.

"You got one more chance," Charlie said, but this time his voice was low, far too low to be heard by the men outside the wooden door. But then, most likely, it was way, way too late for second chances.

The men suddenly stopped pounding on the door, and it was deathly quiet. The littlest babies started to cry.

"Trash," Ava seethed, and she turned her eyes like two drill bits onto Charlie, to let him know it was his fault for knowing such men.

Then, with a crash of breaking wood, the door slammed open, and Martin and the other men stood grinning and wobbling in the doorway, an open jar of likker held out, as if in apology.

As if in slow motion, the drunkards' heads traversed from the rage in Charlie's face down, down to the hammer that swung back and forth, grim as a hanged man, at the end of his bony arm.

They fled. They stumbled over each other and spilt their whiskey, but they made it to their car and piled into it like a troop of circus clowns. And then, feeling safe, Martin cursed Charlie out the window as he turned the key, the motor started and the headlights winked on.

And there in the yellow glow, just a few feet from the hood, was Charlie, a scarecrow come to life in baggy red long-handles, his hammer held high in one fist, like a thunderbolt.

"Help me Jesus," Martin screamed, trying to find reverse.

The car lurched backward and Charlie threw his hammer with all his might, and the windshield shattered into a million glistening pieces. The hammer passed through and hit one of the men hard in the chest, and all three of them piled out, one wheezing, trying to get his breath, the two others cursing and screaming. They ran to the safety of the woods.

Charlie, his face still full of fury, walked into the house and loaded his Belgian 12-gauge, and walked back out on the porch. He stood, patient, until he saw one of the men run for their car, and tracked him across the dark yard like he was a pheasant. There was a half-moon, not good light to shoot by, but good enough.

He squeezed the trigger and the whole house shook, and out in the yard there was a yelp, like when you step on a little dog's tail.

"Damn, you shot me." It was Martin's voice.

"I shot you in the leg," Charlie said, correcting him.

"You still shot me," came the voice from the darkness, followed by some whimpering.

"Well, you ort not to kicked in my door," Charlie said.

For some reason Charlie considered it a point of pride that the men not be able to get back in their car, that they had to walk home. It seemed only reasonable, perhaps, after the trouble they caused.

Finally Ava, who had undergone another sea change, walked up and herded Charlie protectively back inside.

"I guess the law will be here in the morning," he said, all the anger draining out of him, leaving him empty.

"I reckon so," Ava said, and steered him over to the bed.

No one seems to remember what Hootie did, but more than likely he crawled under a bed.

Early the next morning, Walter Rollins came knocking on the door, which Charlie had hung back up before dawn. Walter was a full-time cotton farmer and a full-time police officer in Jacksonville, in Calhoun County, a respected man who did not cheat his pickers and did not complain if the women brought their children to the field. He let the small children play in the cotton wagon with his own boys, and paid in cash.

Walter had perhaps the most distinctive voice in Calhoun County. It was shrill and nasal and strung-out, all at the same time. Walter, a man who liked folks and liked talking, often accentuated the final word in his sentences a long, long time, like he wanted to make it last.

"My God, Char-lie," he said, sitting down at the table and taking a cup of coffee, "what'd you dooooo?"

Charlie told him straight.

Walter accepted a buttered biscuit, and a little daub of apple butter. It was all they had that morning.

"Next time," he said, brushing crumbs off his hands, "why don't ye just kill the little son of a beeetch."

*   *   *

Hootie, because he was weaker, because he needed a hero, brought out the light in Charlie's character. His children pulled it out of him, like taffy, when they crawled in his lap and felt his nose or tugged his ears. Ava could, still, if she wanted, with a cool hand on his sunburned neck. And in a way, sad as it may seem, the likker made him gleam, too, hiding his worries in a golden fog, loosening his tongue, numbing his mind and reminding him it had been a long, long time since he sang "Darling Nelly Gray."

But anger, temper, opened up the door on the hot, dark basement in Charlie's soul. His actions were so quick and so violent that people wondered how the two sides of his character lived in only one body, as if one leg would want to go one way and one leg go another, like a poor zombie conjured from goofer dirt. But the anger, dark as it seemed, was not meanness. Meanness just sleeps inside a man's brain, like a cancer. Anger is put inside a man, spins around in his guts and comes out like bile and razor blades. It looks the same, but only from a distance.

Some people blamed it on the times. Old men swear it even

made the wild things meaner. Men who would have never stolen crept into the chicken houses and stole the eggs, and other men shot at them from the porch. But it wasn't the times, really. The willingness to hurt a man, when that man hurt or threatened you or your loved ones, was distinct, like fingerprints, to each man. In some men, it was tempered by reason and fear, and in others their rage overcame everything in one violent, terrifying moment. Charlie's temper did not blind him. He hit, and hit hard, because he believed he had to.

It is impossible to explain that to someone who has never hit in anger, who has never been hit, and known that the hitting would not end, could not end, until you'd hurt your enemy real, real bad. Jimmy Jim had taught it to Charlie, and Charlie taught it to his boys. Some men sent their children to military school, to learn war with honor. Charlie taught them how to war and win, and to go on living with their heads held straight up.

James learned it when he was about eleven or twelve.

He was on his way to school when an older boy named Dahmer Jones, bigger and stronger, hit him in the leg with a rock. When his daddy saw James limping, he asked, "What happened to you, son?"

When James told him, Charlie just said, "Well, I reckon we can break him of that." He went to a big hickory tree and broke off a limb, and with his pocket knife he made James a big stick—about four feet long and about as big around as his wrist on the big end. "I want to see this stick when you get done with him," Charlie said as he handed James the weapon. "I want to see the bark tore off it.

"And son," Charlie said as his boy walked away, "use the big end."

Later, James told his daddy how it went.

"I went and hid in the culvert, and then I stepped out from it as Dahmer Jones went by. He said, 'Hah, you kind of hoppin', ain't you, Bundrum.' And I set into him, boy, and once I got started I just couldn't stop."

He laid the boy's head open to the skull.

The boys had grown up just like their daddy, unencumbered by too much school or civilization, and Ava wrote them both off as hooligans by the time they were eleven or twelve. His sons, who were becoming teenagers as the 1930s faded slowly into the 1940s, looked and spoke like Charlie, so much so that it was hard to tell them apart at a distance, just three tall, skinny men in overalls, walking the dirt roads and trails.

Charlie had, in the tradition of his own daddy, been hard on his two boys, but they respected him. "My daddy is a man," they would always say when somebody said something about him, about his drinking, his sideline whiskey making, his raggedy overalls. They learned to be men by watching him, the good and the bad.

Like a lot of brothers so close in age, they didn't like each other a lot. They drew blood. Once, in a wood pile, they battled with pine knots, which is like battling with baseball bats. Margaret ran and hid behind the house until it was over.

"They get it from you," Ava always said to Charlie, and he always nodded his head, no high ground to stand on.

But it wasn't hate. If it had been hate, one of them would have died. And, as is often the case, they sided with each other against the entire outside world.

James, with massive fists and arms of bone and sinew, was feared by the other boys. William would pick a fight with two and even three of them, and as they closed on him he would let out a single high whistle. James would come running, and the beating would commence. After a while, it occurred to James that William was whistling a real whole lot, that he was taking advantage of him. So one day, as the whistle came, he just looked up and smiled, and listened as the whistle grew more urgent, then plaintive, then finally faded to silence.

❋  ❋  ❋

The things the boys remembered about their daddy were not always spoken things, which are just wind, really, but things he did. He always walked in front of them on a game trail or through tall grass, so that a snake coiled there would strike at him. He carried a long stick the size of a broom handle, but heavy and green, loose in his hand.

Once, as they pushed through high weeds, they heard a rattler's sing—they only bit you when you walked up on them but that didn't make you any less bit or any less dead—and Charlie and his sons looked around wildly.

A rattler was coiled at William's feet, and it struck even as Charlie stepped in front of his son and whipped his stick at its head, which made a sound like a pistol shot.

The snake thrashed, crazy-like, on the ground, dying, and Charlie kept walking, like nothing had happened, and the two little boys told it to anybody who listened that day, that week, until they led their own kids through the tall grass, stepping in front.

The snake, to Charlie, was just one more thing stabbing at his children, no more evil than drunk men at the door late at night, or an empty flour can or smokehouse. They could all get you, Charlie figured, but could get the children easier, because they were not as strong or fast.

He had to absorb it, like he would have absorbed the poison in those fangs, if that had been the only way to save his son.

He would not have seen it as heroic.

He just figured he could take it.

## 12.

# The worst of it

---

*The foothills*

A half century after the Depression was over and done, I would hear Ava brag about beating it in 1936 and 1937, what she called the worst of it. But her stories would get jumbled up in other remembrances, so it was hard to tell just what all she was telling. The decades ran together in her mind the way the flavors of a two-scoop ice cream cone ran together on your hand outside Tillison's store when I was just a boy, when we asked for a scoop of chocolate *and* butter pecan. She would start out talking about the WPA and in mid-sentence cross over to how she wasn't real sure men ever really landed on that moon and if they did that was the reason why we weren't getting any good rain. It would seem like the original thought had just melted away, like that fifty-cent ice cream, when she would rear back her head and proclaim, "Me and Charlie never did let them babies go hungry, and I'll tell you that and no water hot." I never did know what the last part of that meant, but I knew what the first part did.

They scraped by in 1934 and 1935, and most of 1936. Then, in the winter of 1936, they had some bad luck. They were living in Georgia but Charlie was working on a scaffold over in Alabama, driving nails, raising walls. The scaffold, made from pine planks set on a framework of steel, hadn't been rigged right. He was way up high, reaching in his apron for a nail, when it just fell out from under him.

He hit the jumble of wood and iron hard, on his side, and coughed blood, and the boss man told him to go on home but he worked all that day anyway, because there is a whole lot of difference between a half day and a whole day when they sign your check. A week later, he had pneumonia.

He lay sick for weeks, refusing a doctor, knowing that there was no money for one anyway. He coughed into a rag and sipped now and then on a tonic that was really just white whiskey with a pinch of sugar.

One morning he staggered out of bed and reached for his lace-up boots, but he was still sickly and there was little work then for a puny man. He had lost so much weight that his face looked like a skull. The foremen and the line bosses shook their heads and sent him on down the road. "We need whole men," they told him.

Edna remembers it as the worst time.

"Momma wouldn't eat, but watched us eat, me, William, James and Juanita. We ate cornbread and sometimes we had some peas, and some fried potaters. We lived mostly over in Floyd County then. I remember one day we didn't have nothin' and Uncle Newt brought us over a pan of mashed taters and a hunk of cornbread. Daddy lost his job because he was out so long, then he took an ax and cleared brush for people, and cut pulpwood when they'd let him on the truck, and he would go door to door and ask if they need a well dug, and go stand with the men out at Dixie Clay, in case they needed someone to load the boxcars. And if they did he would load them cars by hand."

Landlords came for their rent, and Ava begged them to let her sew for them instead. She and Edna sewed all day when there was no cotton for her and the older children to pick. Ava counted out pennies on top of the store counters for needles and thread, and had to owe a penny many, many times.

"I'm good for it," she would always say, looking the store owners dead in the eye.

"I know you are, missus," they would say.

They pieced quilts and made sheets and dresses from feed sacks. But it seemed like the day always came when the landlord would walk into the yard and call to them. Mostly, people were apologetic and kind, and some would say how they hated this, but "y'all got to move on." Others were not kind. Just as poverty made some people shine, it stripped the decency from others.

They were living in Coyle's Bluff, also near Rome, when the only way to pay the rent was to sell the cow. Ava led the cow out of the shed and handed the reins to a woman who had come to get it.

"And," the woman said, "I'll take the morning's milk."

Ava had already milked the cow and the woman figured that she was being cheated.

"You can't," Ava said.

"Why?" the woman asked.

"I'm keeping it for my children," Ava said, "because that's all they'll have."

The woman tried to argue. Ava, desperate, might have given in, but she had seen so much of their already meager life shaved away that she just couldn't take any more scraping on the bone that remained.

She turned and walked into the house and portioned out the milk for her children, and watched them as they drank it. The woman huffed a little, then took her cow and left. Ava crowed about that for seventy years.

But that was just Ava. Some days she cried, some days she laughed. On any other day, she might have kicked that woman's derriere back to Rome.

Ava kept the cow's calf, which couldn't give milk now but would in the future. A promise of milk, then, was better than nothing.

A few months later, they ran behind on the rent, again. They were staying at a little place owned by a family named Johnson. Charlie, who had found work a few counties over, was coming that weekend with his paycheck, to square that debt. But the landlord wouldn't wait. He sent a hired man round to the Bundrum house.

"Pay it up," said the man, "or I'm coming back tonight to get that calf."

That night, the hired hand and another man came into their yard carrying a lantern and a rope. James, the oldest boy, had gone with his father. Ava walked out on the porch and begged them to leave them alone, to leave the calf alone.

"It's our food," she said.

William, then just nine or ten, lifted his daddy's shotgun from the wall and stepped out onto the porch before Ava could stop him.

It was a high porch built on narrow columns, what people then called a chicken-leg porch. The two men looked up at the small boy on that big porch holding a gun almost as long as he was, and snorted.

"What you gonna do, boy?" they asked.

"You put that rope on that calf," William said, "and I'll kill you."

The men stopped when William pressed the shotgun's stock into his bony shoulder and pointed the barrel down into their faces. Looking deep, deep into the dark, cold, unblinking eye of that 12-gauge, the men backed slowly from the yard.

The family moved as soon as Charlie came back. Drifters, movers, did not win when landlords brought the sheriff into their borrowed yard in that time. They loaded up in the night, and were gone.

* * *

(I remember all this now when I think about a story I heard once about a student at a prestigious Southern university, a woman who threw away her dollar bills because they cluttered up her room. And one dollar, she said, wouldn't buy anything, anyway.)

* * *

Charlie healed even as the times seemed to get some better, though prosperity is always a relative thing when you're that poor. By 1937 he was working almost every day for whatever anyone could afford. He worked for a side of bacon or a bushel of peaches, and he was able, finally, to go back into the woods and to the riverbanks to shoot game—squirrels and rabbits mostly—and catch fish. He continued to make his whiskey, to drink and to sell. He never would have let his babies go hungry to drink—because that is, and forever will be, the mark of a sorry man, but if you are making it, drinking it just doesn't seem to be such a sin.

He had the skill. His daddy gave him that. All he needed was a quiet place to work. And like his daddy, he soon learned that people—very respectable people—would pay good money for a taste.

In 1937 a new baby, their sixth, was coming. Granny Isom was busy with a baby across the county, so Charlie drove to Rome to fetch that city's town doctor. The doctor asked him, as he crawled into his Model A, if Charlie had any money.

Charlie just told him no, but, well, maybe they could work something out.

# 13.

# Margaret, and mystery

## The foothills

SPRING 1937

They believed that if you ate an onion a day you would live to be a hundred, which may not have been true but at least no one that they knew of ever died eating onions. They believed that burned motor oil cured the mange, even though a dog covered in black oil was twice as objectionable as one with a few bare patches and a constant itch. They believed you could smother a chigger with Vaseline, and that eating too many pickles dried up your blood. They believed things, a lot of things, because their mommas and daddies did.

Just because a man works in overalls, or a woman takes a dip of snuff in the evening, that does not mean they do not hold to traditions. Just as a story passed down through the generations is as precious, as valuable, as bone china, the things we do just because our kin did them are as sacred to us as anything passed along by the gentry. That is why Charlie's behavior on the day his sixth child was born was so puzzling. He turned his back on a tradition so old no one can even remember where it came from, or when it began.

It was a simple ceremony at a birth, once the hard part was over. The baby would be handed to a relative or a respected neighbor or friend, usually one of the eldest, to honor them. Then the relative would carry the newborn slowly, slowly around the house, talking to it, telling it good, fine, hopeful things. They would hold the baby close to their hearts, so the child could feel that beat, and when the circle was complete the old people would give it back to the mother without a word, because to speak about what was said on the sacred circle was bad, bad luck, the same way telling what you wish for over birthday candles will make your wish not come true.

In the foothills, our kin believed that the baby would inherit all that person's goodness, all their finer nature, all the luck, love and talent in them. It did not mean that the baby would not take after their momma and daddy, but that it would have a little something extra from their kin. It was just something these people believed, something they did the exact same way every time because it had always been done the exact same way, until Margaret came.

\* \* \*

She cost Charlie a quart of whiskey, and was born in the season of dogwoods. The doctor in Rome, a man named Gray, delivered the poor woman's baby, a bleating, angry-looking, blond-haired thing that would be beautiful one day but for now looked like a pink rat. Ava insisted on naming her Margaret, for an old woman who had helped care for her once when she was ill, and the boys, James and William, walked around the little house grumbling about one more damn sister. The doctor had a cup of coffee, and didn't offer any advice about child rearing. It seemed like Mr. and Mrs. Bundrum had some experience at that.

Rick Bragg

Charlie followed him out to his A-Model with a quart in his fist. It was a full quart, which is the most amazing thing about that day. It was worth a dollar or more then, in the Depression, and as good as cash and a whole lot better if you were dry. The doctor unscrewed the cap and sniffed but did not take a sip, and if this was an affront, Charlie never said so. A lot of men went blind drinking bad likker, and a few men died. It may seem a sin to trade whiskey for such a thing, but God may have forgiven him that time.

* * *

The ceremony did not happen right away. The baby had to be fed, had to feel comfortable in the arms of its momma. And only then did the baby's daddy pull it from her, then hand it to a great-aunt, or beloved uncle, or man or woman who had been kind to them.

They always said "Thank ye," because it was a gift, truly.

No one knows why Charlie broke with tradition that day—he had not been drinking any—but he scooped the little girl up into his arms and carried her around that tiny house himself, his face tucked into the blanket with hers, whispering something. What, we'll never know.

When he was done he handed Margaret back to Ava, who had not objected when he took her from the bed and did not complain when he brought her back. The other kin who had gathered looked on, a little puzzled. It seemed a tiny bit selfish, to them.

Charlie never said why he did it, and died with it unexplained. We can only guess.

It was not that she was his favorite—he loved all the girls the same, as far as they could tell—and it was not that he thought he was the best person for the baby to take after. Charlie Bundrum knew his failing, his one true failing.

But see, according to tradition, it was only the good things the newborn inherited. This was his chance to funnel all the good, brave

118

and pure things in him into one of his own. It was not science—in science you inherit all the traits, good and bad—just superstition. Or maybe faith.

Still, what if it was true, what if a man could guarantee that his baby would get all the good inside him, and be free from all the weaknesses, and the pain they caused?

What if it was only true?

Margaret was the alter ego of Juanita. She was more timid. She was not a fighter. The fair-skinned little girl with that white-blond hair believed that no matter how mean a person was, they would stop it if she was just patient enough. When other children fought, she walked away. When grown-ups fought, she ran. She fought back only when she was cornered, when there was no way out, and then she clawed and kicked.

Her brothers were mean to her, but they were mean to everyone. They tied her up in sacks, and every time Ava left William to baby-sit her, he gave her a haircut. William cut all the hair off one side and left the other side long, and laughed even when his momma whipped him over it.

When the Bundrums moved from Alabama to Georgia, her brothers told her they were going there to dig up little Emma Mae, who was not dead but buried alive. They gave her a hoe about twice as long as she was, and she dragged that hoe everywhere she went. She believed them, because she was so small, believed that they might not be able to get Emma Mae out of the ground if she was not ready to help them dig.

When someone, a grown-up, told her that they were just fooling her, she sat down and wept, not angry, just sad that they would leave Emma Mae in the ground.

She followed Juanita everywhere. She snuggled up in Edna's lap. Ava always had a needle and thread in hers, and she was always fearful one of the children would run to her and stick themselves on those big needles she used for quilting. Margaret hated the needles.

The needles meant pain, and she hated pain—in her body or in her mind, awfully, terribly bad.

Charlie called her "Pooh Boy," though why no one seems to know, and she would toddle after him down the dirt road to the mailbox, then toddle back, just to be close to him. He was the protector against the pain. When she got a speck in her eye, it was he who laid a warm washcloth against it, to ease the hurt. If she got a burn from their stove, he blew on it. If he caught her brothers being mean to her, he whipped them.

"Maybe we shouldn't write this," she said so many years later, "but I was his favorite. Maybe not in love. He loved us all. But maybe he gave me more attention. I knew that nothing could ever hurt me with Daddy there. I knew he would never let it happen."

# 14.

# Burning

---

Her mind went away while she was on fire.
Margaret was not yet three years old then,
fair and white-blond, a lovely child. They were living in the old Osby
place, maybe three miles from their nearest neighbor, on the Georgia
side of the line. Charlie had gotten temporary work at Fort McClellan
in Alabama, a three-hour drive away, building barracks and roofing.
He slept there, and came home on the weekends. He was gone the
night it happened.

Edna had made Margaret a new dress out of a feed sack, a pretty
dress, Edna said, "but I didn't have no buttons yet, and I told her not
to put it on." It was a long dress, down to her feet. You can grow into
dresses like that.

"I can't wait," Margaret said, and she begged and cried until the
other women in the house, big and little, gave in. Juanita was about
five, Edna was about ten but acted older.

Because Edna didn't have any buttons, they fastened the back of the dress together with a big safety pin. A new dress was the happiest, grandest thing that had happened in her life, and it was her first real, clear memory. How could such a thing wait on buttons.

It was dusk. She and Juanita were cutting paper dolls out of old newspapers, and Ava and Edna were washing clothes on a rub-board not far from the house.

The two little girls made a lot of paper dolls, and the scraps piled up on the floor. Margaret started throwing the paper scraps into the fireplace, and a red-hot coal rolled from the fire and brushed the hem of her dress. The cotton dress blazed up, and Margaret beat at the flames as they climbed the back of her new dress, scorching her legs.

They tried to get it off her, but it fit tight at the neck, where the button would have fastened, and Juanita tore at the safety pin but it wouldn't come undone. Screaming, Margaret ran from the house and onto the porch, and when she rushed out into fresh air the whole dress seemed to come alight. "I was all on fire," she said. It was then that she lost her mind.

Edna and Ava had heard her screams and come running, and caught her just as she breached the door. Ava knocked her to the porch and the two of them started to smother the flames with their bare hands. Edna cried and Ava prayed and cussed and they just beat at the fire until their own hands were blistered, until Margaret lay smoking on the porch, deathly, terrifyingly quiet.

Her eyes were wide, wide open, but she was not seeing anything in this world. She was still breathing, her chest rose and fell, but she was in shock or something like it. It was no so-called near-death experience, just a little child out of her head with pain.

She just remembers that she had a dream.

"I went up and up and I was flying, but I didn't see the Lord. I was playing with these kids, three or four of them, and we could all fly, and we flew all around up there, and we had on white dresses. I flew around a real long time, but I never did see the Lord. I wanted to, 'cause I'd been good. But I'd of remembered if I'd seen the Lord."

They didn't have a car. Charlie had taken it with him. There was no way to get a doctor, at least no way quick. When Margaret came to she cried, and Ava knew then that she was probably not going to die.

Ava had this unusual ability to always do what was needed of her when times were the worst, then panic and crumble. It was so this night. As soon as Margaret was put out, she gently lifted her up and laid her on her stomach—most of the burns were on her legs and back—and started to put salve on them. She told Edna and Juanita to go for help, and finally just gave up and started to shake.

They took Ava's lantern, the big, heavy one, and ran and walked the miles to Miss Osby's, the closest house. Miss Osby didn't have a phone, but she and the girls walked another two miles to a store where there was a telephone. They did not believe an ambulance would come out so far for such a thing, so they called the police in Anniston, Alabama, near Fort McClellan, and they went and found Charlie.

He jumped in his truck and raced home, but when he walked in the door there was whiskey on his breath. Men often took a drink after work, sneaking a few sips of home brew smuggled into the dry counties. But the angels were against him this time. This time, the people who needed him, who believed he could kill any dragon, needed him stone-cold sober.

It would be one of the few times, times his daughters can count on one hand, that he failed them.

\* \* \*

Margaret lay on her belly on the bed, cried-out, quiet again, and the blisters on her lower body had just begun to rise. Charlie stood over her, trying to focus his bleary eyes, and said, "Well, maybe it ain't too bad," and he went to the store and got some more salve, then went back to work.

But it was bad. The blisters rose up big as teacups, and then got infected.

"I used to lie beside her in bed and hold the cover up off her, because she couldn't stand to have nothing touch her, but she would get cold," Edna said. "I had sore hands from trying to tear that dress off her, but that was all right. But sometimes I would go to sleep and drop the cover on her. She sure had it rough. It scared me. I was scared we was gonna lose her."

Margaret would lie there, drifting in and out of her mind, and she would wake up to pain.

Ava sent the girls for Charlie again. This time he saw what had happened to his child through clear eyes, and he took her to the doctor in Rome. He went back to work shamed.

* * *

Many, many years later, I asked her how she felt about it all, if it left any bad memories for her, if it had affected how she felt about him.

"No, hon. I was real young, so it didn't leave no bad scars," she said.

I guess she misunderstood me, that she thought I was talking about the fire itself. Or maybe she understood me just fine.

## 15.

# Gettin' happy

*In the deep woods*

THE LATE 1930S

Likker.

It even sounds like a sin.

Charlie could swing his hammer all day and not make a ten-dollar bill, but he could run off a gallon of white whiskey and make five dollars a jug. He sold it to Jack Milsap, and Ralph Crow, merchants and druggists and other respected men, because his product was clean, because it was pure, and because it was safe as Kool-Aid. Other people may have run it off from rusted truck radiators, their hooch laced with lead salts, invisible, deadly. No one ever found a dead possum floating in Charlie's mash. He never sold a sip—not one sip—that he did not test with his own liver.

Just as his daddy had taken him to the woods to learn it, he took James, then a teenager and his oldest, to help carry wood, to help keep watch. James remembers how his daddy would watch the likker drip slowly, slowly from clean copper tubing—they called that process "sweetening it in"—until it was time to taste.

Charlie carried a clear, flat half-pint bottle in the back pocket of his overalls, and he would run off a pint and shake it to check its bead—good likker had a fine bead of tiny bubbles along its surface when it was shaken. He would peer hard at it, like the bottle was his microscope, then take one quick, hard pull, then a second, then a third, till it was gone.

He would close his eyes and raise his face to the trees, and quietly announce:

"Son, that's alcohol."

He drank exactly one pint for every gallon he sold.

* * *

There was a culture to it, almost a religion, in the deep woods. More than anything, more than wars, or car crashes, or feuds, it killed men of my blood, or caused them to do things that killed them. It was a sin, but it was our sin. I guess it always will be.

Prohibition had come and gone, but most of Alabama and Georgia was officially dry in the 1940s, and would be for decades to come. But it was only dry if you wanted it to be.

In Rome, Anniston, Gadsden and the other cities in the foothills, the wealthier men and women sipped wines and drank stamped brown whiskey that they bought from bootleggers or wet counties. They had it delivered, discreetly, to their back doors, then went to Sunday school stiff-backed, holy-mouthed and straight-faced, as if Jesus didn't know. Some of the old men who had grown up country but now lived in town had a taste for likker made in the trees, and they sought out men like my grandfather.

In the country, every county had at least two bootleggers—one white, one black—and they sold beer by the bottle from trapdoors and wellsprings, to keep it cool, and clear moonshine whiskey by the quart. In Calhoun County on the Alabama side, it was a woman named Aunt Hattie, a legendary figure who gave her customers secret numbers written on bits of paper—a code to make sure that she did not sell by accident to any revenuers or police. Long after she died, and her bootlegging operation had died with her, men kept the scraps of paper with their code in their wallets, and they would pull them and show their number, with pride.

Some people have secret handshakes. We had Aunt Hattie's code.

If you wanted whiskey in the foothills, your likker was almost always clear. It was considered superior to anything from Kentucky, and the fact that it was illegal just made it taste better.

It was a culture of deceit, coursing under the very upturned noses of the hard-shell Baptists and Congregational Holiness of that place and time, a people who got high on the Lord, who walked across backs of church pews when they were enraptured—my momma called it "gettin' happy"—and sometimes even handled serpents to prove that nothing, nothing could pierce the armor of their faith.

But whiskey trickled through, under and around it, invisible—if you did not know where to look.

Even in houses like Charlie Bundrum's, there was a culture of deceit. The funny thing is, it was almost noble.

The deceit was necessary for the making of it, surely, because if a man like Charlie went to prison his family went hungry and that is just a natural fact.

Charlie, like his daddy, went to his still in the black of night, when the deep woods could keep a secret. He never took the same way more than once or twice and always circled and circled his still—he called it his "pot"—like a dog circling his bed before he lays down. Dogs do that, old men say, because they do not want to lay down on a snake. In a way, Charlie was just doing the same thing.

He carried his Belgian-made 12-gauge double-barrel, and a pound-and-half blacksmith's hammer, for snakes, he always said.

Once, twice, they were laying for him, on both sides of the state lines, but he was a ghost in the dark—"walked like a Indian," the cousin Travis Bundrum said. The first time they came for him—the law at that time had to actually catch the whiskey man at his still—he melted quietly into the dark. The next time they were better hidden, and stepped quickly from the trees all around him. He did the only thing he could, he ran over one of them, like a bull over a rodeo clown, and ran the rest of them into the ground. No white man could outrun him in those woods, said his cousins. It is not a myth born from whiskey. It was what people knew, and know now.

If he had James with him and he was suspicious, he would hide him and tell him to lay quiet till he came for him.

They would walk to the still if it was just a few miles from home, and drive and leave the car, a 1935 Plymouth cut-down, if the still was farther off.

James will never forget the time he and his daddy were up high, way up Bean Flat Mountain in the foothills, with about three gallons already run off. That meant Charlie had three pints in him, and, to tell it true, was not seeing all that well. Or else he was seeing double.

It was dusk, heading toward dark, and the fire under the pot was throwing out too much smoke. Charlie always made his whiskey in a cave or under an overhang or in a tangle of fallen trees, so that their branches, like a filter, would help dissipate and hide the smoke from his fires.

But he had put too much wood on the fire, or else part of it was wet, and even with the trees overhead as a screen, the coals sent a fat black column of smoke into the air. James, afraid the revenuers would see it, jumped almost into the fire itself and began flailing at the smoke, till his daddy started shaking with laughter.

"Beat the hell out of it, son," he said, and if any revenuers had been around they would have heard him snorting and belly-laughing there on the ground.

It was, James remembers, quiet and beautiful on the tops of those ridges and deep in the hollows, with no cities to muddle up the stars—just him and his daddy sitting on the grass, telling stories as the fire burned down and the perfume of the cooking whiskey, sweet and strong, ran along the breeze. When he was older his daddy let him have a small taste, and it really did run through his body like blue fire, burning his mouth, scorching his throat, but settling warm into his belly, like good whiskey will. It made you forget things, yes, and made it hard to see things, but nothing worth remembering, nothing worth seeing. At least that was how it seemed after the fourth or fifth swaller.

Sometimes he and his daddy would lay on their backs and watch the stars, which stood still, mostly, unless they had been drinking some, and the lightning bugs, which wandered on the air. The stars were pure white and the lightning bugs were gold, or an electric yellow, depending on the wetness of the air.

That particular night, "just as I finished whupping that smoke," just as the dark settled down completely around them, they saw a single light in the distance, moving slowly toward them in a straight, unwavering line.

"Son," Charlie said in a whisper, deadly serious now, "don't look good, does it?"

James was too scared to speak.

"Step over behind that big pine and stand still," Charlie said. "Don't you move no matter what happens. If it goes bad and they get me, go on home as quick as you can."

Then he stooped over and picked up that blacksmith's hammer, and stood in the clearing by the still, the flames framing him in an aura of yellow light. James wondered, at first, why his daddy didn't hide. Then it came to him.

When the man or men with the light chased Charlie, or fought him, he would be the one drawing all the attention, and James could just slip away—or just stand still, in the deep shadows, until it was safe.

Charlie smacked the hammer once, twice into his palm. It could be revenuers or it could be some low-rent son of a bitch coming to steal his whiskey and perhaps hurt him or his boy. The Belgian shotgun was propped, close at hand, against a tree.

The light came closer and closer and closer and . . . about that time James and his daddy noticed that it didn't seem to be getting any bigger. Then it just hummed right on by, a ball of light, bright, tiny, distinct.

Then, deep in those woods, they knew it was a ghost. Now James knows it was just a lightning bug, but the mother of all lightning bugs, the biggest one anyone has ever, ever seen. But why did it fly so true, for so long? Lightning bugs dance on the breeze.

Ghost stories begin like this. But then, drinking stories begin this way, too.

* * *

Federal men and county sheriffs harried him for thirty years, and while they locked him up now and then for carrying too much moonshine around in his bloodstream, they never caught him cooking.

"They chased him," said James. "I reckon they caught everybody, everybody but Daddy."

He remembers one time, when they were living in Alabama, they saw a big cloud of dust racing above the trees. Two carloads of county pulled up in the yard.

"I don't like this," said James, who was about fourteen.

"It don't make me smile, neither, son," Charlie said.

All eight car doors opened and men poured out. The sheriff—they believe it was the famous still-smasher Socko Pate—walked up to the porch.

"I'm looking for Mr. Chollie Bundrum," he said.

"I am him," Charlie said.

"I'd like to look around your place," he said, "for a whiskey still."

"You go ahead," Charlie said, pleasant, not mocking. Socko was not a man you teased. "If I wasn't gettin' ready to sit down to dinner, I'd go with you."

But as soon as he stepped inside, he turned to James and said, "Son, I believe they got me."

But while the still was just a mile from the house, Charlie had found the perfect place. He had found a deep sinkhole, deeper than a man is tall, and had carefully scooped out a cave in the side of the hole—then covered that with vines and honeysuckle. He had not worn out a path walking to it because he eased through the weeds on a slightly different route every time he went to it.

"Unless he can fly," the sheriff said, walking into the yard, "he ain't been down there."

He called to Charlie to come out of the house.

"Well, we didn't have no luck," he said. "We never found so much as a rabbit trail, all the way up in there."

Charlie told them he would be sure to come and see them if he ever saw a whiskey still close by.

\* \* \*

He could not fly, of course.

But, after a few long pulls on his own product, sometimes he thought he could.

\* \* \*

While a culture of deceit ruled the making of it, it also ruled the drinking of it, for men like Charlie.

Some men drank in their houses, of course. He never did. Ava, who had learned a long time ago that the devil rode on a popping cork, didn't let whiskey in her house. Charlie would not have done it anyway.

131

Under his code, a man did not drink in front of his wife and daughters—but once his boys were old enough, he drank in front of them, and did not lecture them not to drink.

Men drank. Men worked. Men fought.

By the time you were thirteen or fourteen, you were a man, or else something pitiful.

\* \* \*

They drank in the woods, beside their stills, and in their trucks and cars, parked on dirt roads. Sometimes, if they just had to have a tot or two, they would drink parked in their yards.

It was not religion that forced them to hide it. Charlie was not, as we have said, a religious man, though he lived surrounded by people of deep faith. There were men of that time, and this time, too, I guess, who would preach drunk, who would be so full of the spirit—and spirits—that they would stagger to their feet in the woods and start quoting loud and hot from the Bible, until they passed out.

Charlie did not cloak his drinking to hide it from church people. Men like Charlie, the ones squeezed between their love for their families and their love for the likker, came home only when their drinking was done.

That might seem like an empty victory, a senseless one, to have a man drink himself half-blind and then stagger into the house, bringing all the bad things it caused into his home.

But that is one of the reasons they loved him. His nature, his fine nature, was not turned ugly by it. He drank and he laughed and he drank and he sang and he drank and he told good stories, and sometimes he drank and he just went to bed smiling.

He liked living, so he did not drink to hide. He just liked it. He liked the taste.

When he first started making it, as the Depression ended, it was a certain way—as long as he didn't get caught—of making a little money on the side. If he had drank his money up, cheating his family, he would have been a sorry man. But he made that likker and drank a portion of it—and I guess it would be asking too much to expect a man to make it, smelling it, and not have a sip.

I am not trying to excuse it. He did things that he shouldn't have. I guess it takes someone who has outlived a mean drunk to appreciate a kind one.

But he never poisoned anybody. He never caused anyone to go lame or blind from bad whiskey, and if you're going to have whiskey—and it, like the mountains where it was made, will always be with us—you might as well have memorable whiskey. And people do recall it. They truly do.

The one it hurt the most was him.

The law, frustrated at not being able to catch him, dogged him. More than a few police, tired of being knocked upside the head by him when they had tried to haul him to jail for other things, followed him along the dirt roads, and pulled him over when he wobbled.

Once, two Georgia state troopers followed him to a well-known beer joint outside Rome called the Maple on the Hill.

It was a real, sawdust-on-the-floor beer joint, and the mighty Roy Acuff even wrote a song about it—or they named it for the song, one or the other—and Charlie, James and William went in and sat at a row of stools.

The two troopers walked in and stepped up behind him.

"Come on, Bundrum, let's go," one said.

"I ain't doin' nothin'," Charlie said.

"Come on," the other said.

"I'm just sittin' here," he said. "I got these boys with me, and I can't leave 'em here."

Then one of the troopers hooked his arm around Charlie's throat and dragged him backward off the stool.

What happened next in that bar happened so quick that James

and William did not even have time to step in and help him. From the floor, Charlie swept one of his long arms against the back of the trooper's legs and upended him.

"His legs was up where his head was supposed to be," William said.

He landed on his head, and the fight was pretty much out of him. The other trooper took a swing at Charlie with his nightstick, and hit him square and solid across the head—but it just didn't do the job.

Charlie hit the remaining conscious trooper one time in the side of the head, with a sound like concrete blocks slapping together, and the man dropped beside his partner on the floor.

Charlie did not whoop or yell or say a word—the two men seemed beyond hearing, anyway. He dragged first one, then the other, out to the gravel parking lot, and laid them beside their patrol car.

Then he went back inside and drank his beer, until a carload of county deputies pulled into the lot. He told the boys to walk on home—and stepped out to greet them. They beat him a good bit.

\* \* \*

He drove slow when he was drinking, and was good with everything but right turns. He always thought he had a little more room than he did, and was bad to run over the mailbox.

His children would hear his old car rumbling into the drive and—if that was not immediately followed by the sound of sheet metal on tin—they were glad. Over time the mailbox looked like it had been in an undeclared war, and the mailman would slip the letters in and grin.

They were living in Tredegar in Alabama when, late one night, they heard a horrible crash. They ran outside, to see Charlie's truck crumpled against a massive oak tree.

"My God, Daddy," Juanita said, "how did you not see something that big?"

"Well, you see, hon," he said, "there was two of them."

\* \* \*

He would have lived longer, and his wife and children would have had him longer, if he had not been a man who liked his life sweetened with whiskey. His grandchildren would have known him.

But for some men, drinking is like breathing.

He made a living despite it. He never laid out drunk, he seldom slept in the day, the way drinkers do.

I guess you could say he got happy.

\* \* \*

Ava saw it as her job to make sure his hangover was as painful as possible.

"You got to stop, or it'll kill you," she said.

"I know, Momma," he said.

"You got to," she said.

"I know, Momma. I know."

"You ain't even listening to me," she said, her voice rising.

"Yes, Momma, I am," he said.

"No, you ain't," she said, standing over his shoulder, looking down on him like a conscience. Finally he would get up and flee to the yard, and Margaret would follow him, toddling out the door.

"That woman," he would say, "could nag paint off a wall," and Margaret would just sit there, sad, because even a toddler knows when things are wrong.

Sometimes Ava would get so wound up she'd come out on the porch to press her point, and Charlie would climb into his cut-down to get away, all the time saying: "I hear, Momma. I hear."

And then he would be bouncing down the road, safely away, and his penitence would vanish in the dust from his tires.

"He ain't sorry a bit," Ava would say back at the house, and then stomp inside. To Margaret, it seemed like Ava could make the sun sorry for coming up in the morning.

"Why is she so mad at you, Daddy?" she would ask him when she was older.

"Well, hon," he would say, "she's a Holiness."

"What's that?" Margaret said.

"A Holiness," he said, "is somebody who ain't never had no fun."

Ava, he explained, sometimes forgets that she is one, and has some fun before she realizes she is having any.

"She backslides," he explained, "which makes her tolerable."

*　*　*

A time or two, he roofed houses drunk. A cousin told me, grinning, about the time she drove past a big house and saw my grandfather's silhouette on the roofline, wobbling in the clouds.

# 16.

# The letter

*Outside Rome*

THE EARLY 1940S

The letter from the federal government came on a late afternoon in the winter of 1941, when Juanita was eight or nine. Ava read it to Charlie when he came home from work that evening, then went and sat red-eyed by the wood-stove, the government's letter crumpled in her fist.

Juanita asked the older children why she was sad, and they said it was because their daddy had to go to Rome to see a doctor for a test, for a "zamination." If he passed it they were going to give him a green suit like the one Hootie wore, and put him in the army.

Much of the rest of the world was already at war, but that didn't mean a whole lot to her because no one was fighting over their dirt road, their trees. It didn't seem right to her, that her daddy would have to go and leave them alone. Her daddy kept the ha'nts and woolyboogers away. He kept the thunder from knocking down the house. He killed the snakes.

Why couldn't Hootie go, the children wondered, since he already had the suit. They would hate to loose Hootie, but . . .

"We'll starve," said Ava, who was expecting a sixth child, and Charlie just kept saying, hush, now.

Ava was still crying when he got up the next morning to leave. He put on a clean pair of overalls and his denim carpenter's cap, and hugged Ava and the children. He told them not to worry, but even as a small girl Juanita could tell that his face was bleak and grim.

Hootie refused to come in the house. He went and sat by himself in the woods. Charlie called to him but Hootie just went deeper into the trees.

His old truck was broke down, so he left walking. They lived on a hill then, with a long, straight red-dirt driveway. Juanita stood on the porch and watched him walk away. He was still a skinny man—he was thin all his life—and it seemed like he was ten feet tall as he walked away.

"I stayed out in the yard all day and looked down that road, and I guess I looked down it a hundred times," Juanita said. "I didn't say nothin' to nobody. I didn't go in the house to eat. I was just waitin' for him to come back, and I was so afraid he wouldn't. It was the first time I ever remember being sad."

Even as a little girl, she was like him in a lot of ways, skinny and tougher and less prone to cry than any of the girls she played with, a scrapper and tomboy. She didn't cry that day, she just watched.

At dusk, as her momma was lighting the lantern inside, she saw him step into the drive. She ran as fast and as hard as she could, and he caught her up with one hand.

"They didn't want me," was all he said.

She walked back with him, but you really don't have to walk if you are floating on air.

"Momma was still in the house, still squalling," Juanita said. "Momma was always squalling."

At supper, he told Ava what had happened. The doctor had

said he was healthy enough, for a man so thin, but the recruiter told Charlie he had too many responsibilities, that the army was not taking men in their thirties who had five children—and a wife expecting a sixth child. He told Charlie to go home, to be with his family. Charlie told that man he would not duck his duty if he was called, but the man laughed and told Charlie that his sons would soon be old enough to serve, if it was a long war.

"Go on home, Bundrum," the recruiter told him, "to them babies."

\* \* \*

Mary Jo was born on March 27, 1941, on the Georgia side, the last time Granny Isom, who was becoming feeble, would come to Ava's home. Mary Jo, whom everyone would just call Jo, slept in Ava's arms as Juanita and little Margaret stood and stared at her.

"She's kindly ugly, ain't she?" Juanita said.

Margaret nodded her head.

She would grow out of it. Jo would be a daddy's girl, even in a house full of them. As a baby she had terrible earaches, and her daddy bought cigars and blew the smoke into her ears. It was supposed to make it better, something folks believed back then. Whether it worked or not, it is one of her first memories of her daddy, something that helps heal her now, even if it did not heal her then.

\* \* \*

Years later, Jo would say that it was her impending birth, the very fact that she was coming into this world, that made the army send her daddy home.

But Juanita knows that if wishing can make something happen, she wished him back up that driveway, wished him away from a war that took a thousand daddies, ten thousand, from the pines.

"I just couldn't imagine a life without Daddy," Juanita said. "It's hard enough to imagine life without him now."

*   *   *

There was a war coming for them, one that had nothing to do with the Third Reich or the Empire of the Rising Sun. There was an enemy, and when it came, it was riding in a rumble seat.

# 17.

# The Reardens

*Coyle's Bluff*

THE 1940S

The Reardens loved conflict more than chocolate pie. Ned Rearden, who stood almost seven
feet tall and was shaped like a stovepipe, would get into a hideous
cuss-fight with his wife, May, and storm out into the yard. He would
jump into a Ford car and twist the starter and here would come May,
dragging their daughter, Mickey, by the arm, screaming for him to get
out of that car, "or I'll throw Mickey under them car tires." And Ned
would sit and gun the motor to drown out May's screeching, as
Mickey waited nonplussed, catsup on her mouth—she liked to drink
it from the bottle—as May and Ned hollered and the engine roared.
May never threw Mickey under the car tires and Ned never did think
she would, and Mickey at five or six years old was smart enough to
know melodrama when she saw it, and it always ended with the gravel
flying as Ned drove off to Rome, cusses streaming like litter from the
driver's-side window.

Some people are just interesting. They can't help it. They just are.

The Reardens were like that.

About the time Jo was born, Charlie moved his family again, this time up on Coyle's Bluff, near the Oostanaula River. Of all the wild and beautiful places they had lived, this was perhaps the most wild and most beautiful. Deer leapt in front of the car on dirt roads that were little better than pig trails, and skunks lived under the porch, which is a lot like living over a time bomb. But perhaps the wildest creatures there on Coyle's Bluff lived just over the ridgeline from the Bundrums, in a ramshackle house with the curtains closed up tight.

Old Man Rearden, his wife, five grown sons, two grown daughters, one daughter-in-law, a little grandchild with bizarre eating habits and one of the son's sweethearts all lived in a four-room house. Dark smoke drifted from its chimney, even in summer. Unlike most people, who hid a still deep in the woods, the Reardens made their moonshine indoors, and got away with it for a long, long time.

Old Man Rearden was a dried-up little man, in a wheelchair after a stroke, and Ava, whose heart was touched by things like that, made him custard and chocolate pies, which didn't last long in that crowded house. Old Lady Rearden, who was sometimes called Granny Rearden, had the rough circumference of a fifty-five-gallon drum and was almost as tall.

The boys were all dark and tall. There was Ned, the oldest, and Jerry, who was mean as a cornered snake, and Junior, who had nice teeth, and Rodney, who could run like a Tennessee racehorse, and Dan, who was said to be level-headed and likely to make something of himself.

Their daughters were the kind of women who could make a preacher lay his Bible down. June and Ruth were slim, dark and lovely. "They were like movie stars," said Juanita, and men would walk a half day out of their way just to look at them sitting on the porch.

Mickey, the grandchild, was perhaps the most interesting Rearden, even had she not drunk catsup from its source. When Ava would take the pies up to Old Man Rearden, she took Margaret, then about four, with her. As Ava and the Reardens visited in the kitchen, Mickey tortured Margaret by slapping her face just to see what she would do.

Margaret sat and let it happen. Margaret, with her calm spirit, hated no one, and just craved peace. She hated conflict, hated screams, hated curses, hated the fear that a reasonable person feels when other people are trying to inflict pain. Even as a tiny girl, she would just absorb the meanness of the people around her, and as that strange girl slapped her, Margaret literally turned the other cheek.

\* \* \*

"I just took it," she said sixty years later.

"Why?" Juanita said.

" 'Cause I was scared of her," Margaret said.

"You should have told me," Juanita said.

"Why?" Margaret said.

"I would have pinched her," Juanita said.

\* \* \*

Living close to them, back then, was like sneaking under a circus tent. They fought all the time, made whiskey, ran from and sometimes got caught by deputies and revenuers, often escaped, but came straight home to Coyle's Bluff to get caught again. The revenuers there paid absolutely no mind to Charlie Bundrum or his little moonshine still. It would have been like arresting someone for popping bubble gum in the middle of Mardi Gras.

They were the only indoor whiskey cookers the Bundrums had ever seen. Their house was always "black dark" because they kept the curtains closed, said Edna, who was about twelve then. Late at night the Rearden boys would come walking out the front door carrying gallon cans.

Once, on a raid, the revenuers chased Junior and Rodney along the river and caught Junior. They couldn't spare a man to hold him, so one revenuer had him reach his hands around the trunk of a cedar tree, almost as tall as a church steeple, and slapped the handcuffs on him. "He'll not get away unless he takes that tree with him," the revenuer said, and they took off again after Rodney. As soon as they were out of sight, Junior—who was not short on brains—began inching up that skinny tree. A cedar has flimsy limbs, and he just squeezed through them till he got up to the top. When the revenuers got back, he was gone.

The Rearden boys were mostly kind to the Bundrums, except for one, the foul-tempered Jerry. He kept company with a large woman named Norris, a woman with buzzoms the size of feed sacks who was said to be almost as mean as he was, but was treated as part of the Rearden family. Ava would mutter, "Jack Sprat could eat no fat, his wife could eat no lean," if she saw them drive past the house.

Everyone seemed to fear Jerry, except Charlie. Hootie was out-and-out terrified of him, but wouldn't tell why. If Jerry was anywhere around, Hootie stuck fast to Charlie, walking almost under his feet.

* * *

For a year or so, the Bundrums lived beside them. The children even named their favorite hen, a short, plump bird, "Old Lady Rearden," because of that resemblance, and Charlie laughed. "Does look like her," their daddy said.

They love to tell the story of the time a tornado came and they saw Old Lady Rearden huffing and puffing along the ridgeline, trying to make it to a storm pit. But one of her feet slipped, and she rolled halfway down the mountain before she could get stopped.

The Bundrum children laughed, and their momma and daddy scolded them and said it was mean to make fun of people.

The next day, Charlie, grim-faced, walked into the house and said he had some terrible news.

"Miz Rearden has died," he said. "She's out in the yard with her legs stickin' straight up in the air."

The children were stunned, and shamed, but they ran outside to see anyway, because how often does a child get to see a woman the size and circumference of a fifty-five-gallon drum laying dead in the yard with her legs in the air. But when they rushed outside to see her, it was just the hen. She was dead, though. And her legs were, as a point of truth, sticking straight up. "Kicked the bucket, by God," Charlie said as the angry children turned on him, and he laughed half a day. Ava went out, not amused, to see if she was too far gone for dumplings.

* * *

They were good neighbors for the most part. Charlie never made more than a few gallons of whiskey, so he was no threat, no competition, and they seemed to respect the skinny man. All but Jerry. He had a hot-rod Ford, and he would rumble past the Bundrum house and glare.

When a roofing job opened up down on Highway 53, way on down the mountain, Charlie loaded his family and Hootie onto his truck and moved them to a house near the job, owned by a family named Roach. Hootie was much happier there, until one day came when they heard the loud muffler on Jerry's Ford and saw him creep past the house. Norris, all two-hundred-some-odd pounds of her, sat behind him in the rumble seat, like a chubby child on a kiddy car, drinking soda pop and looking mean.

# 18.

# Reckoning

*The Roach place*

THE 1940S

They were getting ready for supper just a few weeks later when Hootie raced up onto their porch, jerked the door open with a crash and slammed it shut behind him, rattling the plates on the table. He shook, and was wild-eyed, like a horse in a burning barn. "Hep me, hep me, Mr. Chollie, he's come to get me ag'in." Then he raced through the house to the back door, snatched it open and was gone in the night.

That was when they heard Jerry Rearden call from the yard.

He had coasted his Ford up to the house, his headlights off, and had almost snatched Hootie before the little man saw him and ran for his life. Now he stood in the gloom with a shotgun pressed into his shoulder. A man doesn't hold his shotgun that way to talk. He holds it that way to kill.

"Send Hootie out," Jerry hollered. "He stole some whiskey from me and I want him."

That was probably when Charlie was sure of what he had suspected all along, that Jerry Rearden was one of the people who had hurt Hootie, to make him tell a secret he did not even know, or just for the sport of it. Hootie didn't have the courage to steal from anybody, and surely not Jerry Rearden. And now this man had come to his house, bringing a threat of violence to where his wife and children lived.

Ava and the girls started to cry, in part from the look on his face, and his boys, now almost teenagers, stood quietly by the windows, looking out. Charlie was a doer, not a thinker, in times like that, but this time he didn't have all the tools he needed to kill Jerry Rearden deader than Aunt Minnie's house cat, which was in his mind to do.

He was out of shells for his shotgun. His hammer and his roofing hatchet were in his truck, in his carpenter's apron, and Jerry now stood between the house and the truck. He looked around for a stick, a lump of coal, anything. He thought about reaching for Ava's iron skillet, but it would have been bad for him, he thought, to get shot dead with a skillet in his hand. That was when Jerry Rearden said he was coming inside, that he was going to take that little son of a bitch and there was nothing Charlie could do about it.

Then Charlie did one of the bravest things I have ever heard of, a thing his children swear to. He opened the door and stepped outside to meet his enemy empty-handed, and just started walking.

"Hootie ain't here," he said, walking, it seemed, straight into the bore of the shotgun. It was a single-shot .410, and he thought that if Jerry didn't get him good with that first shot, he could get his big hands around his throat before Jerry could pop in another load.

"You got to leave here," he said, walking closer. "I got babies in that house."

"You prob'ly a damn thief, too," Jerry said, his voice thick with whiskey, and he pressed his face against the steel of his shotgun to draw a bead. Back then men were always threatening to kill other men. But this man was drunk and mean enough to pull the trigger.

He did.

Inside the house, the girls pulled pillows over their heads, so they would not have to hear the shot, would not have to hear their daddy die.

Charlie felt the hot rush of shot fly past his face, and his legs shook under him with the boom of the gun. But it was a clean miss, and he started to run at Jerry, closing the distance even as Jerry fished in his pocket for another load.

Twenty feet . . .

Jerry cursed and broke open the breech.

Twelve feet . . .

He slapped in the fresh shell.

Eight feet . . .

He snapped the gun closed.

Six feet . . .

He threw it to his shoulder.

Four feet . . .

He saw a fist the size of a lard bucket come flying at his nose.

Charlie was already on him. As Jerry's head snapped back from the blow, Charlie snatched the gun out of his hands like it was a toy and hit him in the teeth with it. Jerry dropped like a box of rocks, his face and teeth a red mess. And just then Charlie saw a huge figure hurl itself at him from the shadows.

It was that big woman, and she lunged at him with a hog-killing knife. Charlie whirled and fired. The woman, who was turned sideways to stab him, took the shot in the side of her breast, point-blank.

The shot passed through the breast and went into and through the other one, and the woman fell hard and heavy onto the grass. She yelled, bled and flopped around, but neither she nor Jerry was mortally wounded and Charlie just stood over them, breathing hard, sweat running like ice water down his spine.

He told them they best be out of his yard before too long, and he walked on up to his house. Ava had not let the children out on the porch, so when the door opened they did not know whether it would be their daddy or the devil himself. He stepped inside to see all of them staring at him with their eyes big, except Margaret, who still had her head covered up.

"We best put the young'uns in the truck," he said, "and go somewhere for a little while."

Out in the yard, they could hear the big woman and Jerry cussing and trying to help each other off the ground. The big woman wailed.

She was blessed that day, that woman, and Charlie was, too. The gun he snatched from Jerry Rearden was a little .410, used for squirrel and rabbit and sometimes deer, not a 12-gauge.

A 12 would have ripped that poor woman almost in two, at point-blank range. But if that gun had been a 12-gauge loaded with buckshot, Rearden would not have missed Charlie in the first place. A man cannot get drunk enough to miss a man with a 12-gauge at point-blank range.

What had happened was not casual. He would go to prison for it, he figured, or the Reardens would kill him. Old Lady Norris was family, almost a Rearden herself for all practical purposes. The fact that there was no wedding ring would not save him.

But he could not have let that man and woman come into his home where two sons, three little girls and an infant would have been in the path of whatever meanness they would bring. That is why he didn't drink his likker at home, why he didn't allow it in his house. It was not, he knew, a perfect wall, but it was the one he had built.

They loaded the children quickly into the cut-down, ignoring the moaning of the two people on the ground, and about that time Hootie just materialized in the yard and crawled on the back of the truck. They rode to a county road, a mile or so away, and waited, but for what they weren't sure, until it seemed senseless to hide, and Ava touched his arm and said quietly, "Charlie, let's go on home." Their yard was empty when Ava and Charlie pulled back into their drive-way, the children asleep in the cut-down. Charlie toted his daughters in two at a time.

The Reardens never came, maybe because they respected him, or because they thought it wasn't worth their time. The law did not even investigate. No deputy ever came into the yard. Like some people need killing, some people need shooting, and need being knocked upside the head.

Charlie never got angry at Hootie for bringing the trouble there, at least that anyone knows of. Ava did. But then Hootie was terrified of Ava anyway, so it didn't change things none. They moved over to Alabama again, not long after that, just for a little distance. But a man with a temper has to drive a long, long way to get away from his nature.

## 19.

# There but for Grace

*Jacksonville, Alabama*

THE 1940S

Grace smoked slim cigarettes, drank like a man and wore makeup, and when she rumbled down Carpenter's Lane in her big car, the people's heads swiveled to follow her, because it was a fine automobile, and because Grace was pretty fine herself, sitting in it.

Grace visited Ava a good bit, when her older sister lived on the Alabama side, and when she came it was like a big movie star had come to town. Grace was a tiny, beautiful woman who went to the beauty shop when she wanted, who dressed in clothes from the department stores in Gadsden, Birmingham and Atlanta. Other women wore bonnets. Grace had store-bought hats with lace that drooped mysteriously over the eyes, hats with silken roses and even tiny redbirds with real feathers sewn onto them, and when she stuck her foot out of the car to get out, there was a high heel on it.

When they were grown, James and William used to take her to

town and pretend she was their girlfriend, to make their sweethearts jealous. She was forty by then but looked twenty-five, and she had eyelashes like bat wings, and when she fluttered them, it just did something to men's insides.

Grace had married a Greek named George Manas, and they ran a cafe in Birmingham and later in Attala, near Gadsden. They were well off—he employed twenty people at one time—and they went to Florida to see the ocean and orange groves and alligators. They sent postcards. Ava put them in the corners of the mirror, so she could look at them.

It was the life Ava could have had, maybe the life she was raised to have. Instead, she sat in another rented house with another baby to feed, to worry over, with two grown sons, a teenage daughter, and two more little girls pulling at her dress, all day, every day.

It was not so obvious, most days, until Grace came and they sat on the porch or in the kitchen, coffee cups in their hands. Grace's hands were still smooth. Ava's, scarred from the cotton bolls that always managed to gouge her up under her nails, and burned pink in places from hot skillet handles.

Her dresses were made from flour sacks and feed sacks, and she picked cotton in them—and it wasn't even her damn cotton.

She wore her hair like the black women of the time, bound up in a scarf, like a turban, to keep it out of her eyes when she did stoop labor and sewing. And one day she unwrapped it and found that the shining, inky black was now cut with white strands, as if by some kind of evil hex, and she cried and cried, and there was not one thing that Charlie could say.

She did not have a wedding ring or even a simple gold band, and while she still had about a hundred cheap, dime-store purses, she didn't have a damn thing to put in them except newspaper clippings of all those things she found interesting but would never do or see, and cutout pictures of Hank Williams from discarded magazines.

She had been a momma, a momma and a manual laborer, her whole damn life, and her husband was not going to lift her out of it and in fact had never promised that he would.

Charlie Bundrum didn't have one pair of overalls she had not had to stitch, and he smelled like tar and snuff, and he drank his moonshine when it pleased him and acted a fool and ran over the mailbox and fought the deputies and brought home hermits.

She could have hated her life.

But what, she always said, if she had married a dull man.

Oh, it was true that she told him to go to hell more times than she could count.

And it was true she told him to get his raggedy behind out of her house before she killed him, and to take his hermit with him.

But no one can remember one time, in all those years, that she told him to shut up.

There was never a time, not one time, that he came in from work, sat down at the kitchen table and had nothing to say.

What a by God tragedy that would have been.

So when Grace climbed back in her car, careful not to snag her stockings, Ava watched from the porch, little girls clutching at her dress, and waved.

\* \* \*

It is why Ava put up with him, and why, about that time, she whipped Blackie Lee. Any woman can appreciate a pretty man, but not every woman can appreciate a talking one.

\* \* \*

One night in Alabama, after the children had been put to bed and Charlie and Ava sat talking quietly in the lamplight, there was a gentle tap on the door.

"Charrrrrrlllllliiiiieeee," came the feminine voice. "Let me in, Charlie, baby."

Margaret and the other girls raised up and looked at their daddy's face. He looked puzzled, and stricken, at the same time.

If it was Ol' Death himself knocking at the door, Charlie could not have looked any more troubled.

"Charrrrrrlllllliiiiieeee," the voice said again. "Let me in, Charlie. It's cold out here."

Ava had taken a minute or two to let the steam build, then she sprang to the door much quicker than she should have been able to, popped the latch and jerked it open so hard the sheer momentum almost flung her off her feet.

"Who the hell is that," she shouted to the darkness outside, and if there had been a woman standing there, right there, she would have knocked her cold as a tater and bounced up and down on her head.

But instead there was just Hubert Woods, a friend of Charlie's, laying flat on his back on the ground, laughing so hard that he could not stand.

He laughed and rolled and laughed and coughed, and further out in the yard his daddy, Earl, laughed, too, and shook his head, and said something about how, boy, you sure are lucky that little woman didn't have no gun.

And Ava just stood there with her fists balled up, but she knew it would be undignified to jump on a grown man while he rolled in the yard, and finally just stomped back in the house and slammed the door.

Charlie, standing on the porch, just looked at Hubert and said, without a smile, "I ought to kill you." Then he walked inside, and out in the yard Hubert and Earl laughed for a long, long time.

The next day, his girls told it over and over and laughed, but they felt sorry for their daddy, in a way. " 'Cause I've never seen a more pitiful look on anybody's face in my whole life," Margaret said.

## 20.

# Sons and daughters

*Calhoun County, Alabama*

THE 1940S

Margaret cannot recall when they went back to Georgia for what would be the last time, or exactly when they came back over to the Alabama side for good. To a little girl, the houses may as well have been railroad cars passing her on a lonely crossroad, as if the houses themselves were on wheels and she was just standing still.

But she remembers the journey.

He banged the gears, and the bald tires on the truck threw dust for fifty yards. Charlie always drove with his large foot to the floor, which would have been dangerous if his old cut-down truck had the will, the heart, to go fast enough to actually hurt anybody. They were going west, through the northwest Georgia mountains, between the wide cotton fields of Cherokee County in Alabama and on into Calhoun County, where Charlie planned to stay awhile, if he could. Ava and Edna sat next to him on the bench seat, Ava with that damn lamp, Edna with Jo riding on her knees. Juanita and Margaret rode in the back with their cow, Buck. Charlie had mercifully thrown a blanket over Buck's eyes before pulling away, for the same reason people cover the eyes of horses when they lead the poor beasts from an inferno. It was an old cow, and the shock might have been too much for it otherwise. He had sent Hootie, James and William ahead, in an old car the boys had bought, and told Hootie to look out for them, which made Hootie shake his head in dismay.

They had stopped in Cedartown for a whole sack of hot dogs, the first time in their lives that Charlie and Ava's children ever had cafe food, and little Margaret, still not yet six, would remember it all her life. The hot dog came wrapped in wax paper, the bun warm and soft, the smell of raw onions, spicy meat and chili filling the car, and she rode the rest of the way full as a tick, mustard on her cheeks.

This was an adventure for her, the longest journey she'd ever made, and she remembers almost every mile of it, remembers looking into a side-view mirror and seeing her daddy wink at her.

Charlie was not an impassive man, but someone whose emotions rode on the bridge of his nose. Happiness, anger, frustration, dismay, disgust and pity—no one ever remembers seeing fear—flashed across his face, depending on the circumstance, but today there was nothing but peace, and maybe contentment.

When Ava was unhappy, nobody was happy. And likewise, when their daddy was happy, when he laughed, they all felt it, and shared it.

He was leaving Georgia, leaving the trouble there, leaving with riches. His children ranged from six feet three to a foot and a half—from soon-to-be-grown men to a baby girl with Shirley Temple curls. Ava and he had stayed together through violence and deprivation, with white-hot words and warm touches, shaken fists and soft forehead kisses. Now, with more than a decade and a half of life lived in small houses, woman and man did not have many secrets left, and what they had discovered in those years was not the love people whisper about over candles, but the kind they need when their baby girl is coughing at three o'clock in the morning. They did not pick and sing as much, now, but when they did, it still rattled the roof.

The Depression was dead, the newspapers said. Calhoun County would be no promised land, but it was growing and carpenters were looking for roofers. And Charlie still had some faithful customers there of his sideline business. The sheriff there liked to bust up whiskey stills to get his picture in the paper, but Charlie had evaded the law before and he believed he would again. He knew the ridges and hollows, knew the hidey-holes.

He made the turnoff to Websters Chapel, and crawled slowly along the road till he saw an opening in the trees, and then went another two miles down a narrow trail, weeds smacking the bottom of the truck, to one more little shack in the middle of pure nothing. Except trees.

"Got us in the damn jungle again," said Ava.

James, William and Hootie were waiting, and the family was not even off the truck good before the brothers launched into an eye-gouging, teeth-rattling, ear-gnawing fistfight, and Charlie had to take his belt off. But the truth was, with them almost grown, a mere belt-whipping was not much of a threat. The boys were in their teens, tall, rawboned, damn nearly indestructible. Prolonged, intense and frequent beatings from Ava, Charlie and—when their arms were tired—other kin had not done much to improve James and William, and the younger boy in particular.

William was still tying his baby sisters up in orange sacks and hanging them from trees and nail pegs, still heaving Margaret into deep water at the swimming holes, to chase off the snakes. A good rock would have done just as well, but he liked to hear her holler when she hit the water. He was not picking on her because she was still the meekest. Edna was too big to be fooled with, Juanita bit, and Jo was too little, and would have sunk. But they did not bruise their sisters, because Charlie would have killed them dead. So they bruised each other.

But as the boys grew ever closer to leaving home and starting their own families, Charlie fretted. It didn't seem possible; it didn't seem right.

Edna was just about a teenager, still the big sister, still serious because she had to be. Ava, as she had grown older in the hard life she chose, had become more mercurial, more prone to fits, rants and weeping jags. But Ava was not one of those Southern women who could afford life as an eccentric victim of circumstance. She did not sit on the veranda waiting for the vapors. Cotton had come back big, after the Depression, and Ava and the older children, dragging the younger ones on their pick sacks, walked the rows and stood in line at the wagon to weigh in for a wad of one-dollar bills.

Edna's responsibilities included sweeping the yard—a lawn was not in fashion then and smooth dirt was the way most people liked it—and when Juanita and Margaret built a playhouse in the middle, Edna did the sensible thing. She tore it down and swept on. A half century later, Margaret and Juanita still held a grudge, still grumbled that "Edna tore our playhouse down."

Juanita was in school now—she loved school—and Margaret used to cry because she couldn't go with her. Jo had grown out of her temporary affliction of unattractiveness—"We sure were glad of it," Margaret said—and would be a beautiful little girl.

All little girls are, but Jo had naturally curly hair, the color of gold, and Margaret used to touch her straight hair and wonder why she had been so sorely shortchanged. At church—where Ava herded all four girls on Sunday mornings—the women used to snatch Jo up and hold her, like a trophy.

They went to the Tredegar Congregational Holiness Church, and the older girls attended Websters Chapel School. When Margaret was six, she went with them. "I couldn't count," she said, "and them kids laughed at me." She would smart from that all her life.

In truth, she could count. She just had trouble saying some of the numbers.

"I can't say 'thirteen' and 'fourteen,' " Margaret said to her teacher, and the words came out—for a reason that is still a family mystery—"hirteen" and "horteen."

The teacher, who was kindly, asked if she was missing her front teeth.

"No," Margaret said, "I just can't talk plain."

"You sound fine," the teacher told her.

"I know," Margaret said, impatiently. "I just can't talk plain when I try to say 'hirteen' and 'horteen.'

"And I still can't say 'vegetables,' " she said, saying it just about right.

The teacher told her a lot of people have trouble with that one.

\* \* \*

It was the first time they ever lived very long in one place in their lives. But in a way they were still movers, still renters, still leasing the dirt they walked on, the birds they heard, the air they breathed.

As she grew older, Margaret wondered why her daddy, a man who could build anything, who made his living with a hammer, never built a house for them, an anchor to hold them in place.

She would come to know that it was for the same reason that the people who cook in nice restaurants do not have dinner in the big front room, and that he built houses for other people's families to clothe and feed his own. But little girls, they still wish for things.

"Daddy worked on some little houses once for the Jim Walter Company, and they put the houses—the very ones that my daddy built—in a calendar," she said. "I wore it out, looking at it. He used to talk about stopping and building us one. He'd say, 'I sure would like to find me some land, maybe by the river.' He said he believed he could rest, by the river."

They lived beside the Coosa and later by its backwaters many times, sometimes within steps of the sluggish brown water. His girls would unload the truck and see the glint of sunlight on the water, and Margaret's heart would always soar.

This might be it, she would think. This might be the time we stop for good.

But it was funny thing, that Depression. History said it was dead and gone, but then history never paid much attention where people like her were concerned. It was as if that death grip on her daddy, and momma, was only loosened. The landlord would still walk in the yard and shout for her daddy, they knew, if he didn't work. But he worked until he could barely stand, and when his car broke down he slung his old tool belt and carpenter's apron over one shoulder and lifted a big five-gallon bucket of tar in his hand, and walked miles to the job.

There ain't no shade on them roofs, he used to say, and the heat, baking through his boots, blistered his feet. A roofer works on his hands and knees, his mouth full of nails, the taste bitter. So Charlie took a dip of snuff to mask it, and at night his girls poured cool water on his feet.

There was never any doubt who he did it for.

* * *

The births of Ava's children spanned two decades, from 1925 to 1944. As James and William were ready to start families themselves, Ava, then nearing forty, gave Charlie one more baby girl.

Sue, who would be the last, was born March 30, 1944, in a house on Carpenter's Lane, just outside Jacksonville, a pretty little college and mill town north of Anniston, the county seat of Calhoun.

The baby was blond, and in a family of pretty girls, she would be the most beautiful—a department-store doll come to life. And her sisters would treat her that way, carrying her around like a toy.

Many of the kinfolks came to witness it, including Grace, Ava's sister. Aunt Grace liked a little toot, so Charlie unscrewed the cap on some likker and poured her a nip in a clear glass—Grace was far, far too ladylike to take a pull on a jug—and by the time Sue came into the world Charlie and Grace were both about half-tight.

"What they doin'?" Jo asked.

"They celebratin'," Margaret said.

\* \* \*

As the war ended in Europe and then in the Pacific, James and William became old enough for the draft. James got his letter one day, inviting him to serve his country, and William hooted, jumped, danced and launched into song:

> *He's in the army now*
> *He's not behind a plow*
> *He's digging a ditch*
> *That son of a bitch*
> *He's in the army now*

He sang it all day. He sang it for a week, and on into the next week. Then the mailman handed William his own draft notice.

\* \* \*

They went to basic training at Camp Shelby, in Mississippi, and Charlie used to go down to see them, to make sure they were doing fine. They were grown, tough men but they were still his boys, and it was the first time that he was not there to stand in the way of real trouble—the first time that they were at the mercy of strangers. So he drove to see them, drove all night, to take them food Ava had sent, to make sure they were fine. It was peacetime then, so he did not worry about a war; he was worried that his boys might not have sense enough to survive the peace.

They did fine. And the army, with all the wisdom of the armed forces, found the perfect job for James, the scrapper who loved a big fight, who loved a drink of likker, who was not concerned with laws.

They made him an MP.

Some of the soldiers, city boys, might have been tempted to poke a little fun at the tall, skinny boy with the jutting ears—maybe even more profound than his daddy's—but James, who could also talk a blue streak, would clamp one giant hand on their necks and look in their eyes with his daddy's stare, and they would do right.

In the lockup, as the angry soldiers threatened and postured, he told them stories about the big stick his daddy once whittled for him to use against a mean, bigger boy named Dahmer Jones, and how he beat that boy bloody with it.

And as he talked he smacked his baton, really just another big, long stick, softly into his hand.

James Bundrum didn't have a lot of trouble in the cell block.

*　*　*

It was a good time, all in all, a good time for the family.

Ava still waited to eat until her children had been fed, but it was out of habit, not because there wasn't enough. It seemed like there was enough of everything then. James and William were coming home from the service, and the new baby was healthy, and the girls were going to school. Times were kind. The federal government was even passing out free peanut butter.

# 21

# Free cheese, cold water and gentle horses

### The Cove Road

THE LATE 1940S

*A shallow well, it gives bad water, muddy water, but that deep well, down in the rock, that water's clean. I can still taste that water.*

—MARGARET, ON THE COVE ROAD HOUSE

Even now, my momma walks the Cove Road in her sweetest dreams.

The woods were old and thick but not endless, the way some of the forests had been that ringed their other houses. Every few acres the wall of trees gave way to wide-open fields that let the sun in.

The house was not a sharecropper's shack or river cabin but had three big, open rooms, and for the first time in as long as the Bundrum children could remember, the family would not all sleep in one room.

It almost drove Hootie crazy. All his time with them, he had squeezed into a vacant corner. Now he walked the three rooms from corner to corner with his tiny hobo bundle over his shoulder, twelve corners to choose from, and he could not decide.

As Charlie and the children began undoing the ropes and lifting their belongings from the truck bed, Hootie was still circling from room to room.

After they unloaded they went out to the well for a drink, and a smile crept across Charlie's face as he tilted the dipper and the water poured down his throat. In almost two decades of motion, they had water that looked like coffee, smelled like sulfur and tasted like turpentine, but never this, so clean and fine-tasting.

Margaret, then about nine, peeked over the edge of the well and down, down. The well was so deep that she could not see the bottom, and the water that came out of it was like ice.

"Make a man give up likker," Charlie said, to no one in particular.

"I doubt it," Ava said.

It was another house without lights, but even though this was just another house way back in the woods, another house where the closest man or woman lived out of earshot, it just had a different feel.

A panther, maybe the very last one that ever walked through these woods, prowled the trees at night. No one ever saw it. They only heard it in the distance, once in a great while. But it only made the blaze in the hearth brighter, somehow, only made the quilts warmer.

In the way people say they sleep better when it's cold, the cat, wandering like a ghost in the dark outside, made Margaret, Jo and little Sue snuggle deeper into their bed. If it got too close, there was always Charlie.

\* \* \*

A yellow school bus came and got them and took them to school, and they only had to walk three miles to catch it, but more than anything about the house, the well and the forests around it, there was a sense, a feeling, that it would last awhile. "We thought we owned it," Margaret said.

Leon Boozer asked ten dollars a month for it. Charlie, who had more work in the county than he could do, counted out twelve ten-dollar bills. Margaret, Ava and the other girls sat almost speechless, because Charlie was committing to one house, one piece of ground. They could not have dreamed it.

He did the same thing every year after that, for an amazing seven years.

Seven years in one place.

"It was our home," Margaret said.

The Cove Road ran through the county a few miles outside the town of Jacksonville. Most people mispronounce its name, and call it the "Coal Road." The house sat a few hundred yards off it, hidden by the trees. The Boozer place was just another rented, borrowed house, but it wove itself into their hearts as if they had paid taxes on it, as if they had the deed rolled up somewhere in a coffee can.

It was not just another floor to walk. It was almost magic.

It even came with a magic horse.

They got the place in an odd way, almost as if there was luck in it. The Smith family had been living there, but they hated living so far out. The Bundrums had lived on Boozer's Lake Road, where Charlie was crowded in by too many houses. The families decided to switch houses, but there was a problem.

The Smiths had a horse named Robert—Robert Smith—and no place to keep him. "Will you take him off my hands?" Mr. Smith asked Charlie.

When the Bundrums pulled up in the cut-down and saw him grazing in a pasture by the house, Margaret squealed.

He was beautiful.

He was black as smut, with one white dot on his forehead, and he had long legs, like a racehorse.

"You was Robert Smith," Charlie said, reaching out to pet his nose. "But now your name is Bob Bundrum."

It seemed too good to be true, that someone would leave such a fine animal, such a well-formed and noble beast, behind.

It became clear, pretty soon, why that had happened.

James's girlfriend at the time was Phine Taylor, a small, dark-haired woman with a lot of Indian blood and green eyes. Phine—they pronounced it "Feen"—was from a farming family close by, and she plowed like a man. Charlie nicknamed her, for reasons apparent only to him, "Tadpole."

One day she hooked Bob up to a plow to get some work out of him, and wrapped herself in the reins, and popped the long leather straps at him and said, "Git up, Bob," and Bob took off like a bullet.

He dragged Phine sideways across the field and out of sight.

"Well," Charlie said from the porch.

Several more long minutes went by.

"Reckon I best go out and see if he's killed Tadpole," he said.

Charlie decided that maybe Bob should be a saddle horse. He put Margaret on his back and began to walk them around the pasture till Bob got tired of it. Then Bob threw Margaret into the fence and trotted off, Charlie cussing him.

There seemed no use for Bob, until Charlie bought a second-hand saddle and climbed up on him himself. And instead of bucking or biting or throwing Charlie into the fence, Bob behaved like a little lamb. Bob and Charlie trotted off to see the neighbors on Sunday, and sometimes, Margaret said, "Daddy stopped off." To "stop off" means to have a toot of likker.

He was not making much likker now himself, and had to go hunting for it, but likker was like chiggers then. If you took a walk in the woods, you would get some of it on you.

And Charlie would sip and tell stories until it was about dark and then he would climb back up on Bob—or someone picked him up and put him there—and Charlie and Bob trotted home, Charlie singing and weaving in the saddle, but at least the mailbox was safe.

And sometimes he would go to sleep in the saddle, slumped forward with his nose buried in the horse's mane, but Bob knew the way home, and Charlie might have been sitting in the backseat of a Cadillac.

But the way Bob treated him when they came into the yard was the magic of it. Bob would gently shrug Charlie to the ground, and then walk slowly off to his stall. The no-name mule, decades ago, had accomplished the same thing, pretty much, but the landing was different. Just getting dropped, Charlie said, was so much better than gettin' throwed.

\*    \*    \*

They had never had a free anything, really, except maybe the fish that Charlie pulled from the Coosa. Now they had a free horse, and free cheese.

If the children thought Bob was magic, they thought that every month, when Ava went into town to get her commodities, was Christmas.

The federal government had discovered that poor people, as tough and resourceful as they were, as proud as they were, would not say no to a little free food.

The government called them "commodities," just plainly packaged surplus food that the government handed out at National Guard armories and courthouse auditoriums, and the word would work its way into the vernacular of the region.

Old women would say they would love to chat, they dearly would, but "I got to go and get my commodities."

It may be the single greatest gift that the federal government ever bestowed on my people. This was not food stamps, which could be used for junk food and white loaf bread and candy.

This was food.

The government handed out cans of good peanut butter, and five-pound loaves of mellow, yellow American cheese. Chances are, if you are Southern and your grandma ever made you a grilled cheese sandwich or a plate of macaroni, there was government cheese in it.

Everybody from the woods got it, if you were old enough or poor enough or had enough children, which was just about everybody. And the people who were too proud to take it would go to their momma's or their grandma's house on the weekends and hack off a pound-weight block of cheese or take a can of peanut butter.

Ava scrambled the cheese in with eggs and the children scraped the skillet. Charlie took a hunk of it fishing, and ate it with saltine crackers and sardines.

The government also handed out big sacks of yellow grits, and cornmeal and flour, oats and rice, and canned chopped meat—people didn't even know what it was but they fried it for breakfast.

Show me somebody who says that their grandma never made them a "sammich" from homemade jelly and government peanut butter, and I'll show you a liar or a Republican.

Even now, when people get together for reunions or Christmas or July Fourth, they talk about that cheese. Country people, unlike fancy, more urbane people, do not think cheese has to smell like a dead dog to be good, and this was clean-smelling and didn't even have any holes in it.

Where I'm from, it almost has its own mystique—because it has been gone so long—like Bear Bryant or Big Jim Folsom or Jim Nabors, who went from Sylacauga, Alabama, to Hollywood, to play "Gomer." Mr. Nabors may not think it is an honor, being compared to cheese. But it truly, truly is.

Sometimes the government went a little far. One day Charlie turned the can opener on a container about the size of a Quaker Oats box, and a whole cooked chicken plopped out.

Everybody just stood around and looked at it.

\* \* \*

The only sadness, in that fat time, was that time could not just stick in place.

They were on the Cove Road when the oldest children left Ava and Charlie to build their own lives. In 1947, in a span of only about three months, James, William and Edna all married. It was like a disease. Ava, Charlie and the four littler girls wondered who it would take next.

James wed Tadpole, which was no surprise. Bob had not managed to kill her.

William wed a lovely girl named Louise Reaves, whose momma and daddy worked in the mill in Gadsden. She was fifteen, with dark hair and blue eyes, and "she always dressed pretty," Margaret said.

And Edna wed a sailor named Charlie Sanders, the son of Mr. Hugh Sanders, who had called for the scripture on that day so long ago, as Jeff Baker bled into his hands.

Edna, Margaret said, had grown into a beautiful woman, with rich brown hair and a lovely face. She had known Charlie Sanders when they were children, and when he went off to the navy they wrote to each other.

Margaret was still a little girl when it seemed like that house just emptied out. She was used to things being a certain way and now it just wasn't so, and it troubled her and made her a little angry.

She was mad the day Charlie Sanders walked up in the yard, that first time.

Listen to her:

"I didn't think he was pretty. She had a boyfriend, William Spencer, and I thought he was pretty, and she dropped him like a cold tater, dropped him like a sack of trash. Charlie Sanders had black, curly hair, tight-curly, and he come walking up in the yard and she just run to him and hugged on him and hugged on him and hugged on him, and I thought she had lost her mind for sure, I thought it was awful. But that was before I knew about Charlie Sanders's heart. That was before I knew it was made of gold."

Juanita was now the oldest child, which was just as well, Margaret said, since she had always been bossy anyway.

*　*　*

It was as hard for the older children to leave as it would have been for a planet to break free of the sun. The tie was still way too tight, too strong, to the man and woman who had raised them.

James and Tadpole moved a mile or two, Edna and Charlie moved over the ridge to Tredegar, and William and Louise moved to the dark side of the moon. They went off to Gadsden, a thirty-minute drive if the police in Glencoe did not catch you just as you crossed the Etowah County line. It was like the house on the Cove Road broke into four pieces, and the pieces landed right close by.

*　*　*

They ate at each other's kitchen tables, and as their own babies came they grew up with the smaller children of Ava and Charlie, so the houses shook with laughter and dripped with tears and the babies were handed from lap to lap, and all the old stories were told over and over again. The grandchildren called him "Paw-paw," and he liked that.

He was a young man then, just in his forties. He was still thin, and when he bought a cheap dress coat to wear, it looked like he forgot to take the hanger out, it hung so loose on him.

Ava no longer had to make her dresses from flour sacks. She was a frugal woman, though, and she bought clothes for herself and the children at rummage sales, in Anniston, Gadsden, Jacksonville and Piedmont, a dime apiece for dresses, skirts and blouses, and the little girls always knew what they would be wearing in a year or two by looking at the backs of their sisters.

There was not much money to waste, and when they splurged they usually splurged on food.

They still talk about the Sunday morning breakfasts, about how Charlie would wake up early and start slicing meat, ham or fatback or country steak, and Ava would pat out the biscuits, about the size of a granny woman's palm. She greased the sheet with lard, so that even the bread had the smell of bacon in it. And when she pulled the pan from the woodstove they would be golden on the top and pale yellow on the sides, and even cold they were pretty good, and in the afternoon people who came to visit would ask politely if she had any biscuit left.

She would butter some and leave some plain, and sometimes the children would slip a little piece of commodity cheese inside, to let it melt.

Bob would smell the biscuits when they came out of the oven. He was never penned—there was no need since there was really nowhere for him to go—and he would trot over to the house and wait.

If it was summer and the windows were open, he would stick his head in the window and Ava would stick a biscuit in his mouth, and Bob would swallow it down and wait for another, but biscuit, Ava would say, don't grow on trees.

But the thing they loved most was the link sausages, and the song that went with them. Because they didn't have a refrigerator, Charlie had to buy some of the breakfast food that morning. He would wake early, real early, and drive to the store. He would stop at Y. C. Parris's store or at Ed Young's and buy links made from pork, about as big around as a banana and with skin almost as tough as what came on the original pig.

It was spiced with garlic and red pepper, and he would slice it longways and fry it in bacon grease, and as it sizzled Charlie's girls would sing a song they learned from Mr. Hugh Sanders, whom they had come to call Grandpa Sanders in his old age.

> *The butcher threw a sausage*
> *Down upon the floor*
> *The dog said "I decline"*
> *For in that link, I recognize*
> *That dear ol' gal of mine*

The coffee would boil, the smell mixing in with everything else, and Charlie would begin to make the gravy. Ava would make grits, and fry up a mess of eggs, and twist open the top of a jar of preserves, and they would eat like rich people, only rich people don't really eat this good.

* * *

Sundays was for church and loafering. If Ava and the girls went to church that morning, Charlie went the other way.

In the afternoons the kinfolks would come by or they would go to them. Grandpa Sanders had become part of their family and they became a part of his, and the children would crawl all over him.

He would sit in the shade, a baby on his lap, the other little girls clustered around, and sing in a plaintive, miserable tone:

> *Go tell Aunt Sally*
> *Go tell Aunt Sally*
> *Go tell Aunt Sally*
> *The old gray goose is dead*

And the little girls would start to cry and even the baby's lips would start to tremble, and Grandpa Sanders would just shake his head in sorrow and sing on:

> Wonder if they been saving
> Wonder if they been saving
> Wonder if they been saving
> To make a feather bed

And the children would fall about the ground, sobbing, and Grandpa Sanders would sit looking innocent as the mommas glared at him.

It seemed like the windows always had tomatoes in them, soaking up the sun, getting ripe. It seemed like the men were always walking up from the riverbanks with strings of fish. It seemed like the babies in all four households were growing up fat and healthy, like the big mills always had openings on the day shift and the fort always needed a woman to sew or a man to drive a truck or a bus.

The steel was rolling again night and day in Gadsden, and William got on right away, and James and Charlie had homes to build and roof and others to tear down—it always bothered Charlie that a man could get a paycheck just as big for ripping something down as he did for putting it up—and on the weekends there was visiting, feasting and storytelling, and a little drinking and banjo picking, and just enough fighting to be sociable. And when a dark cloud drifted over, all eyes still cut to him, expecting him to purse his lips out and blow it away. Sometimes he brought the cloud with him, but they always seemed to forgive him for that.

\* \* \*

He hadn't changed much on the outside. His face was still mostly unlined as he passed forty, and his hair didn't fall out, and his teeth stayed white and straight, and his little girls were proud of him. Time just seemed to bounce off him, somehow. He could still climb a scaffold like a monkey, still drive a ten-penny nail with one measured, massive, dead-on blow, still make a man's eyes water with the power of his grip. He could still drink likker like water.

Time had been harder on Ava, but that is the way of it. She had given birth to eight children, buried one, raised half of the ones that survived, and was now raising the other half, with white already in her hair. Her legs were cut with little white scars from wading through the briers, because she was too much of a lady to pick cotton in pants. Her face was already seamed, and she wore old-lady bonnets in the fields, a baby sometimes on her hip.

It should not even have to be said, really, but her children loved her, and her new grandchildren did too. She was unselfish, and she loved them back. And while a lot of people say that they gave a life, their complete life, to family, she could back it up with every line, every sunspot, on her neck, face and hands.

The worries, for her husband, for her children, for survival in the bleak years, had piled up in her mind, and she got lost in it, from time to time, the way some people do. But she always found her way out, somehow, always found a way to push through that dark curtain, and when she came out of that trance she would smile, this beautiful, beautiful smile. It was almost worth it, when she went away in her mind, to watch her come back from it. It was like flipping the light switch on in a flower shop.

She did not compete with Charlie for their love, the way some mommas do. She was far, far too busy, and too damn smart, for that.

She knew he had their hearts, mostly.

She knew, as much as anybody in the whole wide world, how he could break them.

## 22.

# Do like I say, not like I do

---

*The Cove Road*

ABOUT 1948

The night James decided to kill George Buchanan, Charlie was in the yard, enjoying the
night air and looking at the stars a little bit before he went in to bed.
You could see the stars on the Cove Road, clear and bright just like
when he was a boy on that bad mule riding in from the big city of
Gadsden. He was not a smoker and he didn't like to dip right before
he went to bed, so sometimes he just went out into the yard and stood
in the quiet, especially if Ava was emotional that night. Sometimes
Hootie walked out with him and waited on him to say something, and
if he didn't that was fine, too. And they would stand and listen to
crickets and night birds, and Hootie would talk to them awhile.

Charlie was alone that night, standing so quiet and still that
James did not even see him slouching there, in the shadows, when
James tiptoed into the house to get a gun.

It was a good thing he was there, good for James, good for the
Bundrum family, and especially good for George Buchanan.

It happened this way:

James, Phine and their first baby, Mary, were between houses and living with Charlie and Ava then. James had gone out drinking that night with George, which was his first poor decision of the evening, "because everybody knew George was mean as a snake," James admitted.

George Buchanan was about the only man anyone knew in this corner of the country who'd had his throat cut and lived. He was a big man with squinty blue eyes and chin whiskers, and a man not to be messed with.

As they pulled up in the yard in George's Model A, he looked over at James, who was about twenty-two then.

"You got any money on you, Bundrum?" he said.

James said he didn't have none.

"You a liar," George said.

James just got out and slammed the door and George drove off, but with every step he made to the house his rage ticked up a little, getting hotter and hotter. By the time he touched the screen door he knew that he had to kill George. It might not have been his conclusion if he had been sober and clear-headed, but he wasn't. He quietly took the shotgun off the wall—everyone inside was sleeping—and went back outside.

He checked the gun. It was loaded with double-aught buckshot. It could knock a deer down or blow out a man's chest.

George only lived a little piece off and James figured to walk over there and kill him, but he had barely made it off the porch when he heard, almost in a whisper:

"Hey, boy."

He saw his daddy standing in the moonlight.

"Hey, Daddy," he said.

"What you doin' with that gun?"

"I reckon I'm gonna kill George," he said.

His daddy didn't say anything.

"I'm mad," James said.

He started walking and his daddy fell into step beside him. They walked down a little hill, and Charlie told him to hold up a minute.

"Son," he said, "you got a wife and a little baby in that house."

"I know," James said, "but—"

"I said you got a wife and baby in that house," Charlie said, not used to repeating himself.

"But," James said, "I—"

Charlie hit his son as hard as he could across the jaw with his clenched fist, hard as he could because that boy was as big as him now, and as strong, and because he intended it to be the last lick passed in anger that night, or in love.

James's head snapped back and his arms flew out and Charlie took the shotgun as his son fell backward onto the ground. To James, it was like lightning hit him in his jaw. It burned for one hot, brutal second and then he went to sleep. He was sleeping before he hit the ground.

He woke up a little later to see his daddy there, still looking at the stars.

"I said," his daddy began, as if the punch had never been thrown, "that you got a wife and a baby now, and if you'd killed him, you'd be gone."

To James, it seemed like the words were coming from very, very far away.

"They'd put you in the penitentiary," Charlie said, "and who would take care of them?"

He helped James up and they went back to the house.

"If you ever do anything that damn dumb again," Charlie said, his hand on his boy's arm, "I'll leave you for the buzzards."

At home, James bled a whole lot onto a pillowcase.

* * *

It might seem a little hypocritical. If George Buchanan had ever called Charlie a liar, Charlie might have killed him on the spot. But it is one thing to beat on a man in anger and another to shoot him when he steps out on his porch. Charlie understood the finer points of the law, as it applied to poor people and drinking men.

He also had more than forty years of life to look back on, at the mistakes, at the violence he had seen, had dealt out and had survived. He had seen its consequences, and stood humbled before judges, hating it and counting his sentence off in his mind, wondering how many groceries Ava had, wondering—his mind working quick—if he would be out before they had to do without.

Some people would call it a complicated existence, would wonder how come he did not do right all the time, and spare himself and his family that drama.

The answer is that if he had, he would have been somebody else.

As he got older, he thought things through more. He used what people remember as a pretty fine brain more than his knuckles. But the truth is, sometimes it takes both.

He could have reasoned with James that night, and in fact he had honestly tried, but it was just a mile or two to the Buchanan place, and every step they took closer to it was one more step he might have had to carry his son back. Most men, hit by him, didn't come to that quick, but hitting James was like punching himself, and he knew how hard his head was.

* * *

"Knocked me out, cold as an onion," James would say, when it came up on Sundays and Christmas Eve and around the campfire. "If he asked you something, you was supposed to answer him straight, and I forgot that, that night. And he always said that if you ever hit any-body, hit 'em hard, and I reckon I forgot that, too. But things like that, once your eyes can focus right again, make you love your daddy. I know everybody loves their daddy, I know you're supposed to. But there I was, a grown-up man, and he was still saving me. Now, ain't that one hundred percent man?"

# 23.

## Lost

---

It is not a family that will talk for long about sadness, and on some days, sadness is all there is. James's two smallest babies died when his and Phine's house burned that year, while he was at work and she was at the neighbor's home. Mary and Jeanette, the two oldest girls, crawled out a window, but a boy baby, James Junior, and girl baby, Shirley, died in the black smoke. "It was the worst thing that ever happened to us," said Margaret. That is the most anybody said about it in fifty years, and about all there is to say now.

# 24.

# Holy Name

---

*The Cove Road*

THE EARLY 1950S

Margaret didn't mind being up so high, for the same reason a baby laughs when you toss it in the air.

"We helped him roof, me and Juanita, when I was about twelve or thirteen. I wasn't scared being so high because I knew he would stop me if I fell, and it didn't scare Juanita, because it just didn't. Nothing did much. But Daddy wouldn't take us with him to roof if he was roofing in town, because men would holler at us, and Daddy didn't like that."

Juanita was a teenager then and tough as a prison bantamweight, but slim and dark-haired and pretty, which is why Charlie never let his two teenage girls help him roof in town. It must have been a sight, though, the rawboned man in his baggy overalls kneeling up high on the skyline with the pretty dark-haired girl working on one side of him and another, fairer daughter swinging a hammer on the other side. He would fill his mouth full of roofing nails and spit one nail, just one, into his open hand, and seat the nail with one lick. That way, he could keep one hand partly free to snatch at one of the girls if they slipped.

* * *

He got out of bed slow one morning, feeling weak, like he could barely raise his arms, let alone a hammer. At the job, when he tried to climb the ladder, he made a step or two, and just sagged. He drove home from the job, but when he pulled up in the driveway he sat awhile behind the wheel, holding on to it. Margaret, who was twelve or thirteen then, was not even born the last time he had been sick, when the scaffold fell on him. All her life, he was not just healthy, he was bulletproof.

Now he went bone white from the pain in his insides, and couldn't eat. He told Ava he had to see the doctor at Holy Name of Jesus Hospital, and he would drive himself over to Gadsden in the morning.

As he got ready to go, Charlie looked at Margaret and said, "Pooh Boy, why don't you ride over there with me and we can stay the night with Riller and Tobe"—his sister and brother-in-law, who still lived in Gadsden. And Margaret wondered why, if they were just going to see a doctor, they would need a place to stay.

She didn't really want to go, because hospitals were sad places and sick places, and Holy Name was a Catholic hospital, run by the strange Catholic nuns. But she was glad her daddy asked her to go, so she crawled into his old car with him and they headed up the Gadsden highway.

Her daddy walked into the hospital but didn't come out that night, or the next. Only the nuns came in and out. To Margaret, they looked like angels, but that did not make her feel any better.

Riller, now on her way to being an old woman, and Tobe, who

had retired from the steel plant, sat with him in the hospital. But Charlie told them he didn't want to scare his daughter, so every night she sat in the car in the hospital parking lot and waited.

She spent her days with Riller, and her aunt sent her on errands. One day Tobe's false teeth tore up—Margaret can't recall exactly how a person tears up a set of teeth—and Riller sent Margaret to the repair shop with Tobe's teeth wrapped in a napkin.

She walked with the grinning teeth held way, way out in front of her, because sometimes the napkin slipped off and the hard pink part, the gum part, brushed her hand. She hated that, and she wished her daddy would hurry and get well. But one thing was certain. She never had any use for false teeth after that.

She was lean and light-skinned and her hair was almost white, and it hung completely straight. Jo had got all the curls, and Margaret would rub her hair between her fingers and wish it didn't just hang there the way it did.

But mostly, she just wanted to be brave. She wanted to be just like him, fearless like him, but she couldn't be.

"You couldn't scare him, but I took after poor ol' Momma, and Momma was scared about all the time, unless you made her mad. I always wished I could be fearless. Because I hated it, being scared. Juanita was just like Daddy. She wasn't scared of nothing, and I guess she never was. I wish I could have took after him, like Juanita took after him. She's more like him than any of us. She got the guts and the backbone. She just copes with things. But fear, Lord, it works out on me."

She tried to act tough. "I wore pants, blue jeans. Juanita grew up in pants."

Juanita, she thought, wouldn't be scared to go into the hospital and see about him. Juanita would have waltzed right up to the doctor and said, "Hey, you." Juanita would have bossed the nurses around.

But Margaret just sat in the car, wishing she could play the radio but knowing it would run the battery down, wondering why her daddy didn't just bust through the hospital doors and take her home.

And of course, one evening, he did. "And then me and him went home and he went back to work, and nobody thought much about it."

As the years went by, she learned that he had gone to Holy Name because of his liver. It was bad. The doctor cut part of it out.

A lifetime of moonshine whiskey, the only bad habit he had except for fighting and a little snuff and some discreet cussing, had rotted his liver, and a man can't live without a liver. But he can live with part of one, the doctor had told him, if he gets off the likker, and stays off.

Margaret just knew her daddy was home, and that everything was fine again, the way Juanita knew it would be fine on that day, a whole decade before, when she had seen him walking up the dirt driveway from his trip to Rome to see the army men. It wasn't like he was a ghost of the man who had walked into the hospital, the way some people are when the doctors carve on them. He was the same man as before. He worked as hard, and fished as much.

\* \* \*

He seemed to spend more time with them after that. He taught the two oldest girls still at home, Margaret and Juanita, how to drive, before their legal age. He would pull his car to the side of a road and get out, letting whoever was in the middle slide under the wheel. He did not sit there all tensed up, but laughed as the girls ground hard on the gears and meandered from ditch to ditch, trying to see over the dash, and Hootie, who still rode in the back, wondered if he was about to see angels.

Hootie was still with them, still under Ava's disapproving gaze, and Charlie's protection. He still helped Charlie roof when he wanted to and still just sat on the porch or in the deep woods when he didn't, and got a little older and maybe even a little uglier, if it was possible.

He and Charlie still went to the river to set out trotlines, and every time, he hung back a little when it was time to load up and go home, like there was something calling to him there, and probably there was.

But he had been around so long that he was more than just family, he was almost a stick of furniture. He still didn't have much to say but he still handed out dimes, and the littler girls sat by him on the porch, the way the older sisters had.

It was about that time that Charlie took in a young couple named Souther. They had just gotten married, and the boy was saving up to rent a house and had no place to stay. The boy was a carpenter, like Charlie, and was working the same job. Charlie told him he had room in his little house, and they stayed until they got on their feet, and then moved on.

One night, a young man Charlie knew staggered up and passed out cold on their front porch, and Ava walked out and stared down at him as he snored peacefully on the planks. She cut her eyes to Charlie.

"We ain't keeping him," she said.

But the word was out. Sometimes a good reputation can be just as inflated as a bad one, but everyone in that part of the world learned of the man's kindness, and people, people in need or in trouble, just seemed to drift his way. They stayed a night or a month or, like Hootie, decades. It is not as romantic, maybe, as his reputation for making good likker, or for laying grown men flat with one good lick, but people still mention it from time to time.

\* \* \*

The years had scoured him on the inside, but you couldn't see that when you saw him standing on the roofline, his long body framed by the clouds, that ever-present hammer swinging, swinging. Some men act old, as if they are practicing for their last years, practicing for dying. Charlie did not act old.

He was in his forties and already a grandfather, with a telltale scar above his liver. He had shot men—and one large woman—and smacked them with hammers. It routinely took a carload of deputies to put him in chains, and if all else failed, he could pick a fight with Ava.

He never seemed to get, or want, a lull in the adventure of living, as if he knew that old age was something he would never see. It may be why he seldom took a nap.

# 25

# Lying still

*On the Coosa*

It had rained. It used to rain every afternoon in the late summer back then, but it doesn't anymore. The old people say it's because we've cut down all the green.

It was still green that day, and the air was so wet it stuck to you when you moved against it, like fresh paint off a wall. Charlie, wearing a pair of overalls but no shirt, dripped sweat as he poled a homemade boat between the walls of trees that leaned in over the river, leaving barely a sliver of space for the hot sun to cleave in and sparkle off the water. For Travis Bundrum, Claude's boy and Charlie's great-nephew, it seemed a wild, dank and dangerous place, and the sluggish water seemed to have no bottom to it as Charlie felt for the sand and rock with the end of his long pole.

The boat rode low in the water because Charlie had filled it up with kin. Travis was eleven then, his brother Sonny was about four-teen, and their cousin Roger was nine or so, and they had all begged to come. Travis's daddy, Claude, had spent time in the TB sanatorium, and had not been able to take his boy on many fishing trips like this.

Rounding out the party was Travis's uncle Rich, Claude's brother, who sat with the boys and let Charlie do the navigating, and most of the work. Richard was a fine-looking man, with sandy hair and blue eyes, who was said to be tenderhearted. He was a talker like Charlie, and was one of his favorites. The boys sat between the men in the middle of the boat, and tall tales and yarns whizzed back and forth over their heads, like bullets.

But as they headed up the river in that boat, which seemed to dip and wallow with every ripple, Travis, especially, wondered if he had been wise to come.

"We passed under branches that grew right over the water, and Uncle Charlie slapped at them, with the pole, to see if they had any water moccasins in them. The snakes would drop right in on you if you didn't. There was water oaks and scrub oaks and pines, and deep pine thickets that lined the banks. There was bootleggers' shacks all up and down it, open drinking and gambling, and you knew some hard men lived there.

"But I knew Uncle Charlie would take care of us. He just seemed, natural, I guess, on it. He was a mysterious man to us in a lot of ways, and he handled that boat expertly, and he knew the Coosa, every mile of it."

Charlie was a hero to Travis, because he fought men and won and lived life pretty much as he damn well pleased, and because other men seemed to respect and admire him, and said so. People said he could stand so still in the trees that the squirrels would forget he was there and—quick as anything—Charlie would reach out with his hand and snatch one and knock its head against a tree before it could bite him, and stuff it in his coat pocket. People said they had seen him kill rabbits with rocks and hunks of lead. People said a lot of things. Travis had never seen any of that but he knew that when you went with Charlie to fish, you actually caught fish, instead of sitting on the bank wishing that you had.

To Travis, maybe to a lot of people, Charlie fit better in the past of the river, of these foothills, than in the here and now. The new blacktop highways, reaching all the way from the mist-covered hills to the wire grass and lowlands to the south, signaled the region's future. Charlie, who still used a broken branch as a fish stringer, was its history.

His boats were never store-bought. He still made his own boats from car hoods, and this time he had taken the hoods off two 1940 Ford coupes and welded them together to form a fat, stubby canoe. This day, Charlie was taking the kinfolks with him to set out his trotlines.

Trotlines are the way a man fishes when he is more interested in food than he is in sport. Charlie would take a long string and, every foot or so, tie a line and hook on it, and bait each one of the hooks with the cheapest, most foul-smelling stuff he could find. They would use mussels dug from the sandbars, or spoiled cow or hog liver, or chicken guts, or pieces of carp—trash fish—or even moldy bread, which men squeezed into tight balls so it would not melt off the hook quite so fast.

Then he would stretch the long line across the river or a tributary or deep pool, and let the river carry the fish past it.

Sometimes, especially during the Depression, he needed some fish in a hurry, and he would carry an old crank telephone with him, the type that you had to twist the handle round and round to make a call.

Twisting the crank built up an electrical charge, and after he had turned its tail a few times he would drop the line in the water to shock the fish, and they would come floating to the top, along with an assortment of snakes, turtles and other living things.

Charlie would scoop up the fish and turtles—turtle soup was a fine thing then, even if you were not hungry—and leave the snakes. It may taste like chicken, as some people said, but it probably also tastes a little bit like snake, and even a little bit is a reason to gag.

The game wardens frowned on the shock method of fishing, but it was hard to catch a man at it. To this day, the rusting remnants of old crank telephones lie at the bottom of that river, covered up in a half century of silt and muck.

Charlie had quit all that a long time ago, and now he was fishing legal. They had a foul-smelling bucket of innards in the boat, and planned to bait a trotline, spend the night on the riverbank and check it in the morning. With any luck, they'd have fish and hush puppies tomorrow.

Early in the evening he found a place to camp, just below a rickety old cabin set up high on a bank, and Travis and the boys sat around the fire and listened to the men yarn.

"We had a meal of sardines, crackers and Vienna sausages, and just before dark Uncle Charlie and Uncle Richard walked over a footlog and up the hill to get a quart of whiskey. It was a full moon, and it was almost like daylight."

When the two men came back they let the fire burn out and tried to get to sleep, but loud cussing coming from the bootlegger's shack up the hill woke up the ones who had actually been able to shut their eyes. Even though there was a good moon, it seemed like the heart of darkness to the boys.

"It seems like everything was magnified in those woods," said Travis. "Then this loud argument started up on the hill, and you could hear cursing and the sound of licks being passed, and then there was a shot."

The boys jumped up, but Charlie told them, quietly, sternly, to hush, boys, and be still. Then, up the hill, the shack's door swung open.

Down on the river, the three boys moved in close to Charlie.

"The men come out, and two men were carrying a body

wrapped in a tarp," Travis said. "I guess there was six or seven of them in all, and as the two men carried the body down to the river, the others stood and looked down the bank, like they were looking for something."

That was when Charlie tugged or pushed the boys down to the ground, hissing: "Lay down, and shut your mouth."

"We didn't hesitate," Travis said. They just dropped, and buried themselves in the shadows and in the leaves as the men carrying the body walked right on past them, and the men up above them scanned the bank for witnesses.

The men weighted the tarp with rocks, heaved the body into the river with a loud splash and walked back up the bank, and again Uncle Charlie whispered for Travis and the boys to lay still now, and patted them gently with his big hands.

And though it would have felt better to just get up and run for it, to go crashing through the trees, there was Charlie's hand pressing them down, down.

They had, for all practical purposes, witnessed a killing. The kind of men who casually murdered one of their own and fed him to the catfish without even a glance back, let alone a word to the Lord, would, Travis knew even then, not hesitate to kill three wide-eyed boys and a couple of fishermen.

"So we just laid there, and we laid there all night," with his heart hammering at his chest for one hour, two, three and on and on and on, until finally just before dawn Charlie figured the bad men were passed out, asleep or gone, and they crept to the boat and glided away.

The men must have figured that Charlie and Rich were passing by and had stopped for some likker, then just moved on, not that they were camping right there, that they had heard the shot and seen them weight and sink the body.

And for a lifetime Travis Bundrum wondered what if, what if the men had walked right up on them, or smelled the woodsmoke or the empty sardine cans, or seen the boat pulled half in, half out of the river.

But he never wondered why he lived through it. He survived that night because his uncle Charlie, even with a pint—more or less—of likker in him, held him down in that groundcover with the power of his voice, his hands and his will.

\* \* \*

Charlie went back to the river not long after that and put out his lines, and this time he caught some river cats and mud cats, which are yellow because they hug the bottom where the sun never shines, and tossed them on the bank.

He gutted them on the river, throwing the innards into the water, and finished cleaning them on an old board stretched across two stumps in his backyard.

Edna, who was the best fish cooker in the family and probably in the United States, took over, and dusted them in cornmeal and salt and black pepper, and fried them just perfect, so that the outside was crisp and the inside was moist and flaky, with enough of what people called a whang—a bit of a muddy taste—to tell you it was real food.

She fried potatoes—what they called Irish potatoes—and made the best hush puppies that have ever been, the kind my momma cooked for me. They would take the meal and mix in milk or water and diced onion—sometimes green onion if it was summer—and maybe even a little cubed-up commodity cheese. But instead of deep-frying them in little round balls, they would spoon it out in the hot grease in an iron skillet, in little patties.

And sometimes they would send one of the boys to the store to get a block of ice, and they would chip it up with a butcher knife and put it in a tub with some Coca-Colas or Royal Crown or the brand Double Cola, if the Georgia kinfolks had driven over to see them. It is one of the great mysteries of life that Double Colas could not be bought this far into Alabama—you could only get them over the state line in Rome. Sometimes they would lay a watermelon in the ice water, to let it get cold. But there was never any beer, because drinking is a sin.

And they would eat it all and sit and talk and sometimes someone would even pick and sing a little, or Grandpa Sanders would tell a tale. They would talk until it was too dark to see, and then they would talk to the dark.

The children played hide-and-seek in the wet grass, and chased lightning bugs and put them in a jar with holes poked in the lid, but they never did shine all that much once you put them under glass.

\* \* \*

The town of Jacksonville was growing. The jail, made from rock, was still the most imposing structure on the square, and the Confederate soldier still watched over its citizens with granite eyes.

But you could buy everything from a suit of clothes to a vanilla float there. The Creamery sold a big ol' scoop for a nickel, and Juanita—who always got vanilla—would drag Margaret in there by the hand, a dime scorching her fingertips. She was about seventeen then, and Margaret a little younger. But with ice cream in their hands, they were little girls all over again, and they would sit and watch the cars. You never saw a mule anymore, not in town.

If they had money, they went to the theater on the square and saw a cowboy movie, usually with Roy Rogers and Dale Evans and Trigger, but if Dale's horse had a name they cannot remember it now. Tarzan of the Apes swung through the trees and must have killed the same big ol' snake and the same stuffed crocodile a thousand times, but they liked to sit in the back and munch a nickel bag of popcorn and listen to him yell. "It was the best popcorn I've had in my whole life," Juanita said.

It was not Charlie's world anymore.

The revenuers had airplanes now, and took a man's picture from the sky. Sheriff Socko Pate was in the *Anniston Star* almost every week, it seemed like, him and a bunch of deputies standing over another busted still. Charlie made a last few gallons to sip on for posterity, then stripped the copper tubing from his still to sell as scrap and left the rest of it to rust away in the woods. Practically every other whiskey man in north Alabama and northwestern Georgia had done time for making shine, but he just retired, quietly and undefeated.

It wasn't the same in other ways. The state troopers seldom had to chase a man anymore down the dirt roads. They just took down his tag number and sent a car out to fetch him when they felt like it. That, to Charlie, was just mean.

A man couldn't drive drunk now with all the cars, all the cars that went so fast on the creeping blacktop, and if a man fought the police or the deputies in an honest, bare-knuckle fight, it almost seemed as if they did not appreciate the contest in it, like they lost their sense of humor as soon as he balled up his fist. Taking a whupping from Charlie had been almost a rite of passage for a lot of young troopers, deputies and police, but now the men behind the badges pulled their batons and put a hand on their pistol—and what fun is that.

A man didn't do a night in jail anymore to sober up. They took him to the county lockup in Anniston, and it cost good money to bail him out, money his family didn't have. The judges still knew his name, still shook their heads and sometimes even smiled every two or three years when the tall man stepped before them, a man without malice, just a dusty old code of behavior that sometimes ran sideways with the law. But more and more, as the city limits inched out into the country, the law penned him in.

There was one trooper in particular he didn't like—which was a shame because the man's wife was a nurse at Piedmont Hospital, and helped deliver Charlie's grandchildren—and when he arrested him, Charlie just refused to ride with him in his patrol car. Charlie would go sit down and wait in the ditch for another trooper to drive all the way out and get him.

For Ava, the changing years brought an end to that cursed gloom, as even poor people got their houses wired for electricity. For Charlie, the Tennessee Valley Authority was no blessing. It changed his river to create huge backwaters that swallowed houses and pasture fences and old barns, and pretty soon city people were building second houses on the banks, and "fish camps" that had electricity and refrigerators and radios that blared out into the darkness.

But there were still a few wild places on the water, and Charlie went to them when he felt it all pressing in on him.

He never told his family about the killing. They heard about it only after his death, from Travis.

\* \* \*

Such a thing will haunt you till your hair turns gray, and it did that to Travis. "How strange it was, that it wasn't mentioned after that, by Uncle Charlie or Uncle Rich. But I thought about that man. I wondered who he was, if he had a family, but it was just a thing we didn't talk about."

Several years after it happened, Travis and his uncle Rich were out in the yard talking about nothing in particular. And out of the blue, Travis said:

"Uncle Rich, they killed that feller, didn't they?"

"Yes, son," Rich said. "They sure did."

And they never talked about it again, and Travis didn't talk about it at all, until he heard that a cousin was writing a book about his uncle Charlie, and he thought it was time.

Sometimes, when he rides around the square in Jacksonville and sees the Confederate statue there, he thinks about how someone should chip one out in Charlie Bundrum's likeness and put it up there, to keep the other one company.

He thinks that if people really wanted to honor someone who was part of this place, about this place, someone who had courage and heart, then Charlie would do just fine.

The Creamery is gone. The theater is gone. And men like Charlie are gone. Why not, he figured, erect a statue to a man in a pair of overalls and a long-billed carpenter's cap, a hammer or a trotline in his hands and a clear pint bottle in his back pocket.

He does not believe that will ever happen, of course. But imagine if it did, if all the beloved men were cast in stone and propped up there, an army of men in overalls and jumpers and hobnailed boots, holding hammers and big wrenches and bolls of cotton in their hands. An army of grandfathers, frozen in the act of baiting hooks or opening a can of peaches with a pocketknife.

Imagine that.

## 26.

# Hello, and goodbye

*Jacksonville*

He was standing on the square in Jacksonville the first time she saw him.

"What a pretty little man," Margaret thought.

His hair was slicked back and almost black, and he had striking blue eyes in a face that was Cherokee dark, his cheekbones high and his nose a little hooked. And he looked like he could be mean, if he wanted to be, but mostly he just looked good.

He was thin and slight but powerful-looking, like Alan Ladd, and he had on a black suit and a starched white shirt and a skinny black tie, and black loafers with dimes in them. He had a cigarette in his lips and he slouched on the corner, like he was somebody.

Her boyfriend at the time was a friend of the dark-haired boy, and had borrowed his car that day to take Margaret to town.

When the boy with Margaret saw the dark-haired boy on the corner, he pulled up to introduce him to his date.

"This is Charles Bragg," her boyfriend said. "He's a marine. He's going to Korea here, pretty soon."

Charles took her hand.

"This is Margaret," the boy said.

She was still barely in her teens but tall, almost as tall as the dark-haired boy, and already she was what most people called beautiful.

The straight, pale hair she hated so much hung to her shoulders and she had a look that people could not describe, a serene look, but a fragile look, too. Her face was perfect, and she smiled hello.

He was too cool to say much then, it seemed. "He just smiled this wicked little smile, and I saw he had a little flower in a buttonhole on his coat, and I didn't know why," Margaret said.

But he was not being suave, he just forgot how to talk for a few seconds. Later, much later, he would say she looked like a movie star.

She got to know the boy a little bit, but there didn't seem to be a future in it. She didn't know much about Korea—the truth is, most people here didn't even know where the place was—and no one had ever heard of a "police action" before. But he had told her, told everybody, that he was leaving this little town, that he wasn't gonna work in no damn cotton mill for a lifetime, like his daddy did. Even if he came back home alive, he was gone for good. That made some people sad, people who had loved him for a lifetime, or just a little while. But he asked Margaret, later, when he came home on a furlough, if she would mind if he wrote her a letter every now and then, and she said it would be fine, if he really wanted to.

## 27.

# Underwater

You had to sneak off to do it, but you did it. You had to be able to swim the river, or the other boys would make fun of you. It was not so much that you had to do it to be a man, you had to do it to be a boy. So boys of eleven and twelve tugged on a pair of cutoff blue jeans, lied to their mommas and went to the widest place, or the narrowest, and waded in up to their waist. They would stand there, arms, face and neck burned red or brown, and let that river run through fingers as if they were divining its intent. And then they would push hard off the sandy bottom and grab a double armload of water, and beat and kick at it like a bad dream till a finger or toe scraped bottom on the other side. The ones who did not make it, who got pulled too far downstream by the current and got too tired to fight it anymore, got their picture in the newspaper.

The dams made a different river. The dams made a river so wide, so deep, that a boy just stood on the man-made banks and hoped he didn't fall in.

The big dam, built in the winter of 1939, made a whole new world. Men used big, three-pronged snatch hooks to drag out monstrous catfish, almost as long as a man, and fishermen told stories of cats that lay like submarines at the base of those dams, giants lolling in the currents, too fat to move. Even accounting for how much a fisherman will lie, those were damn large fish. Charlie caught one cat about three quarters as long as he was, and was so astounded he took it home and had his picture made.

To Charlie, a river was supposed to run narrow and wild, and was supposed to change in size and speed and character when it rained, or in drought, and should never, ever be so wide a man could not cross it on a footlog—a tree that had fallen in a storm, creating a natural bridge. But though he never liked what the dams had done to the landscape, a big fish is still a big fish, and as that water pooled he prowled its banks, hunting.

It seemed like the fish just swam right up and jumped in a man's arms there. The fish were too big for a conventional rod and reel, so he used an old pool cue and fixed a strong snatch hook to his line, which was about as thick as nylon cord.

They called it snagging. As the giant cats, buffalo, jack salmon and other fish drifted past near the dam, he dropped his hook right down on them.

He didn't do it for sport, for there was precious little sport in it. He did it for the meat—that's what they called it, the meat—and it is doubtful that he ever wasted a fish.

He was a social man and liked company, but this was a bloody and methodical process, so he either fished with Hootie or fished alone. One spring day, he threw his pool cue in the backseat of his Dodge and told Ava he'd be back, d'rectly. The Dodge had a faulty starter, but it fired right up and he took that as a good sign. Fishing, despite what some men will tell you, is about luck, and Charlie believed in it.

He wanted Hootie to go but no one could find him, so he rolled his window down and stuck his big ol' knobby elbow out, like he always did, and left them in a swirl of dust.

\* \* \*

Guntersville, Alabama, is one of the prettiest places on earth, as you approach it from the riverside. The water is not sluggish, not brown, but clean-looking like the ocean or the Gulf, and flocks of big white birds, hundreds, maybe thousands, swirled over the lake.

Charlie found a spot to park right near the water, and took his tackle over to a place near some granite rocks, and peered over into the water, waiting for the big ones to coast by.

Later, as the sky started to darken, he noticed how high the river seemed to be running, so much higher than before. He was always intrigued at how the light-bill barons always seemed to be saving up their water or letting it go, based on everything but nature, and it had been that way since the damn thing was built.

He also noticed that it was clouding up something terrible, and that the sky was changing from blue to a deep and angry purple, like it was bruised. Then the rain came at him like a waterfall.

He ran to his car through the mud, and noticed that he couldn't tell anymore where the bank ended and the river began. He jumped in and tried the starter, and the thing whined and groaned but wouldn't catch. Starters do that when you need them not to.

He tried it and tried it, the rain pounding and pounding at the roof, and the starter got weaker, fainter, and the water just got higher, higher . . .

\* \* \*

In the vernacular of the time and place, the words "I'll be back, d'rectly" mean the absolute opposite of how they sound.

There is nothing direct about it. It means that a person will be home for supper, unless they stop off for a swaller, or drop by kinfolks' houses, or the fishing is particularly good. But Charlie didn't have any fancy ice chest to store his catch, so he always came home no later than the morning after.

When he didn't come home the next morning, Ava and the girls were not particularly worried, but as the day wore on and he didn't pull into the driveway, they started to wonder what was keeping him.

Ava figured he had found somebody with some homemade likker and was just waiting for his eyes to focus before heading home. By nightfall she was positive of it, and by dawn of the next day, after pacing the floor, she prayed to God it was that, only that.

He had been gone for two days, and had not sent word. Margaret, Juanita and Juanita's boyfriend, the son of the sawmill owner and a good boy named Ed Fair, drove all around the back roads, thinking maybe his car had just broke down.

Juanita told James and Earl Woods—it was Earl and Hubert who had played the joke on Charlie that night they pretended to be a woman at the door—and James and Earl drove up to Guntersville.

The river was still in flood, but was starting to recede. It had swallowed Charlie's car.

When James and Earl found it, it was still covered almost to the top of the roof with brown water.

James felt around inside, feeling for his daddy. But there was no body. Up the bank, caught in some bushes, they found his pool cue and his tackle.

It put a tremble in the people who loved him, and Ava, when they told her, began to cry. Then she just went and laid down, facing the wall.

Her brittle mind, a mind that had been chipped and flaked by so many worries over a lifetime, cracked a little then, and the fissure ran, longer and longer, every day he was missing.

Margaret, who was sixteen or so, went and sat by herself, numb.

It was worse than when she sat waiting for him in the hospital parking lot. It was worse than anything.

But the men who knew Charlie could not believe that a river had killed him, even a man-made river where the water piled up against a giant cement wall.

They searched the riverbanks, afraid of what they would find, but while there were dead chickens, dead cows and knots of snakes, there was no man on the mudbanks or sandbars or snagged in the dead trees.

They checked all the hospitals and the morgues, but no one who matched Charlie's description had been brought in. Then, out of common sense, they started checking the jails. They enlisted the help of what these Alabama Bundrums called the Georgia people, the kin over there.

Together, they called or drove by every jail for a hundred miles on both sides of the line. Some places, the deputies just said, "Naw, we ain't got him," because they had had him before. Others ran down their lists of inmates. Nothing. The first week passed. His children were frantic.

In town, people asked Margaret: "Have they found your daddy yet?" And she would shake her head and cry.

Friends helped, and even people who barely knew him. They even called the Birmingham jail, though it is nowhere close to Guntersville and Charlie would have had no reason to be there. But everybody knew about Birmingham, about the jail there. A poor man, a man dressed raggedy or dirty, was swept off the street.

Commissioner Eugene "Bull" Connor didn't want any white trash on his streets, and officers routinely swept the street and the bus station for vagrants. But when James called to ask them if they had his daddy, a bored clerk ran down the docket and said they had no one by that name in the jail.

Two weeks had gone by since he went missing. As a last resort, James drove to the jails and police stations to plead. He even went to

Birmingham. He asked again for a Charlie Bundrum, and a woman asked if James would spell it for her, and she traced her finger down a list.

"B-U-N-D-R-U-M," she said, and then her finger stopped.

"We've got him," she said. " 'Vagrancy.' "

James didn't cry or act a fool. He knew his daddy had not drowned. Snapping turtles didn't drown. Water moccasins didn't drown. They could, but they just didn't.

He asked the woman, politely:

"Can I have him back?"

\* \* \*

They took him home, but the word had already reached the family. When they saw their daddy step from the car, they ran for him, but froze, just froze, at the fury on his face and the storm in his eyes.

\* \* \*

When the car refused to start, and with the flood coming, he left it and walked in the rain to the bus station. The only way to get home was to buy a ticket to Birmingham, and then to Anniston or Gadsden.

He stepped off the bus in Birmingham with no baggage, in tattered overalls—he always wore his worst pair to fish—with fish blood, and worse, on them, and a work shirt worn through at the elbows.

He planned on having a cup of coffee. He was not drunk. He was not even drinking. He was just trying to go home.

He was sitting on a bench, near a group of other ragged men who had stepped off the bus in Birmingham, when two carloads of city police carrying billy clubs came moving fast down the sidewalk where he was waiting for the bus, and swept it clean. He was charged with vagrancy. He had a pocketful of hooks and a can of snuff and a dollar or two, and had no way to make his bail. They didn't give him a phone call. They just made him a guest of what would be, a few years later, the most famous jail in the country.

The calls to the jail were answered by someone who apparently had no idea how the name Bundrum looked when it was written down.

So he just waited, and seethed, and hated it, because there wasn't a damn thing he could do about it.

They had power over him in a way no man had ever had, and it burned a hole in him. He had been in jail before, but every time until now, he had by God earned it.

\* \* \*

It took days for him to cool down. In the meantime, Ava came back into the world of the living, and his daughters rejoiced, and the word of his miraculous discovery spread on both sides of the state line.

"That was when I learned to pray," Margaret said. "I promised the Lord a lot of things, if he would let my daddy come back."

\* \* \*

Just as Charlie could always find a wild place to fish or set out his trot-lines, boys found places to swim the river, places where the fear was small enough to challenge. I know, because I stood in it with them, a feeling of dread in my guts, my hands searching the ripples for a promise that it would deliver me, breathing, to that other side. And for a while, when you feel the water carrying you sideways as fast as you can pull for the other bank, you really are stuck halfway between life and death, and as close to being in purgatory as a Protestant is likely going to be.

Leave it to Charlie, to my grandpa, to be the only man I know who was said to be lost in it, then come striding back, big as life, into the here and now. It wasn't the same as Huck and Tom faking their deaths just to hear the cannon boom across the Mississippi, to attend their funerals. Only Charlie could be presumed drowned and it turn out he was just short on bail.

# 28.

# Pilfered roses

---

*Jacksonville*

1953–1955

The dark-haired boy stole flowers for her when he came back from the war.

He would be driving down the road and see a rosebush, and stomp on the brakes and almost send the people with him through the windshield. Since the war he had carried a straight razor in his slacks pocket, and he whipped it out like a saber as he ran into the yard. Quick, he would slash the stems and come sprinting back to the car, and spin the wheels in the getaway.

Once, he was riding beside Margaret's daddy in his truck when he saw a huge rosebush on a steep bank, and he said, "Stop, Charlie, stop!" and he was out the door before Charlie could say a word. He climbed the bank and came down with a giant armload of red roses.

Charlie hung his head, because he had never stolen a thing in his life and now he was an accessory to the theft of yard flowers, but as the boy climbed in and slammed the door he didn't have the heart to seriously chastise him, because he knew where the flowers were going.

The boy had come home from the war a whole man, or at least that was how it seemed, and Margaret was just happy he had come home at all. He didn't talk much about all the killing he had seen or done, he just stole flowers.

He seemed to have lost his desire to leave the town where he had grown up, or maybe he just found a reason to stay. He still wore a black suit every time he came to see her, and he came to see her a lot. "And if he ever had his hand held behind his back when he walked up the walk, I knew I had some roses," she said.

He was a little bit of a smart-aleck, "and always acted like he knowed everything." But every time she got mad at him, here he would come with his arm behind his back, grinning.

She asked her daddy to find him some work so he could stay out of the cotton mill, and he did. The boy was respectful to him. Charles Bragg didn't know a damn thing about being a carpenter or about roofing, but he listened and he learned. Charles met Charlie at his house in the mornings and rode to work with him. There was never confusion as to names. Charles was only called Charles. Charlie was never called anything but Charlie—in fact it was his legal name. Mostly, Charles just called him "sir."

Charlie couldn't get the boy to be careful, though. He walked the rooftops, no matter how high up, completely unafraid, and Charlie figured that a man who had seen people shot to pieces overseas was not too scared of falling off a roof, even though it could make you just as dead.

One day they were putting up a new roof—not just the shingles but the plywood base—and Charles slipped and fell through a hole in the roof. He just managed to catch the corner of a board with his left hand. He couldn't reach across his body and get a grip with his other hand, so he just hung there, by one hand, till Charlie could get to him.

"I'll say this much for him," Charlie said to Margaret, "the boy's strong."

He said something else, sometimes, about him.

"He misses his war."

He liked to fight. He picked them. He fought like a rooster fights, from something deep inside that has to be turned loose, before it burns a hole.

And they barely touched him, the men he fought. Where Charlie had just clobbered men, Charles bloodied them and danced away, untouched. The Corps had scarce use for a man who couldn't fight, and Charles had pulled two hitches.

The boy drank, too, but Charlie didn't have much to say about that. If the worst he ever did was get drunk and get caught pilfering roadside flowers, or pick a fight now and then, he might not be all that bad. In spite of himself, he liked Charles.

But Charlie had lived long enough to know that rage was never something that could be aimed straight and true like a Remington, but something that blew up and hurt people every which way.

So day by day they worked on the rooftops and he watched him and listened to him—the boy didn't have much to say, though—and if Charles ever went bad, he would be there to knock a knot on his head, or run him off. But instead the boy was respectful to him and Ava and very kind to his daughter in his presence.

One day Charles came walking up in the yard literally dripping with flowers, flowers of every kind, a bushel or more of them. Charlie, who was not a stupid man, knew what the boy had in mind.

"Did you ask them people if you could cut them flowers?" Margaret asked him as he proposed.

"Sure," Charles said.

\* \* \*

Charlie and Ava lost two of their daughters in 1955, one to a boy who wooed with flowers and one to a boy who wooed with a coal truck and assorted milk chocolates.

Hoyt Fair's boy, Ed, was still courting Juanita. Hoyt was a well-known, respected man, a Congregational Holiness minister. The Fair family had run the sawmill, and now his sons ran the coal yard. Ed was a round-faced boy who always gave Juanita a big heart-shaped box of chocolates on Valentine's Day. He had finished high school, and had a gray Chrysler. But sometimes he came straight from work to see her and drove the coal truck, and sometimes the Bundrums would load up in it and they would all go over to Edna and Charlie Sanders's house to watch television.

Nobody worried about what kind of husband Ed would make. He was a good boy and everybody knew it, who didn't drink and worked hard and made a good living. If he stayed out late, he was coon huntin'.

He was the kind of Southern man who expressed his toughness with tools. He broke down dump-truck tires with a sledge and chisel, and when he needed to see if a car's electrical system was hot, he just grabbed a wire to see if it shocked him. He could weld, plow, drive a bulldozer or a front-end loader, run a power saw, work the boom on a pulpwood truck without killing anybody, and drink RC Colas by the crate.

Juanita and Ed got married first, in Mississippi. Juanita came home to Jacksonville with a solid man—and an unlimited supply of really fine tools.

* * *

Margaret and Charles got married not long after that. Her daddy told her he was happy for her, but she couldn't understand why such a tough man would have tears in his eyes.

Ava was suspicious of Charles.

"He drinks," she said.

## 29.

# Jeanette, Child of God,
# and the Flour Girl

*Jacksonville*

THE 1950S

He called Edna's second-oldest girl, Linda, Flour Girl, because she would take the lid off the flour barrel when no one was looking, to play in it. She would eat a little of it, but mostly she just liked the white cloud it made when she threw it in the air. Edna would walk in to see her two big eyes shining from what seemed to be a white mask. It is hard to beat a child at times like that, but she tried.

Back when she was still a toddler, the Flour Girl would come running when her grandpa Charlie came in the door. Instead of jumping onto his legs the way the other grandkids did, she would stop a few feet in front of him and just stare, up and up and up, at the tall man.

"Is that my girl?" he would say, and then he would bend over from his waist, with that incredible balance any roofer has to have, till his nose was inches from her face. To the little girl it must have looked like a crane dropping from the sky.

Then he would just stand there, bent more than double, his hands on his hips, and grin, and she would squeal.

He could carry two and sometimes even three at a time, if one rode his back and looped their arms around his neck, and it was hard keeping them out of his pockets and his snuff can. When he would take a dip the babies would sneeze, and he laughed at that. The bad thing about snuff is you have to have a spit can—for him, it was usually an empty can of pork and beans, washed clean—and the bad thing about grandchildren is that they are always, always, going to kick the spit can over. With as many as he and Ava had, the spit can was in constant peril.

By the time he was fifty, he was covered up in grandkids. They rode his bony knees and swung from his arms and legs and pulled his ears, which is exactly what he wanted them to do.

The babies that his son James had lost to the house fire had been among Charlie's first grandchildren, and when they died he had balled his fists and pounded his own legs and cursed God and man. Edna said she had not seen such misery in him since he buried his own little girl, Emma Mae, so many years before.

But as the years tumbled by, his older children filled his house and his yard with little boys and girls, and while he never forgot that tragedy, the grandchildren who came after it created a soft, warm distance, or at least that was how it seemed.

James and Phine had Mary, David, Jimmy, Jeanette and Linda Faye, and William and Louise had Peggy, Alton, Janie and Becky. Edna and Charlie Sanders had a house full of girls, with Betty, Linda, Elizabeth and Wanda. Juanita and Ed had Jackie, a girl, then little Joe Edward. But the baby boy died when he was just a few months old, a reminder of how precious and fragile this family, his family, could be.

\* \* \*

Juanita went to the boy's grave every day.

One morning, her daddy gently took her aside.

"As long as you go," he said, "it'll hurt."

He knew his daughter could not push the child from her mind, but he knew that standing over a grave is no way to get on with living.

"For a while," he said. "Don't go for a while."

\* \* \*

They all went to him when it hurt. The grandchildren learned early on to run to him when the dog bit, or they got slashed by a brier. He was there the day that James's boy David fell and cut his throat on a fruit jar—it wasn't as bad as it sounds—and at a hundred other little emergencies.

Like Margaret, they just figured he could fix anything. It was why Jeanette wasn't afraid the day she fell out of the Dodge.

Charlie, Ava, Jo and Sue were living on the Roy Webb Road then, not far from Holder's store. Charlie was sitting on the porch, feeling a little lonely.

"I think," he said, "I'll go get James's kids."

He did things like that. When things were too quiet, he would just stride to the car and go loafering, and sometimes he came back with grandkids hanging from the truck bed.

This time, he had David, Jimmy, Mary and Jeanette, who was then six years old, in his 1946 Dodge. He was rounding a curve when the door on the passenger side just flew open and Jeanette, who was sitting next to the door, fell out.

She rolled and tumbled and then lay in the middle of the road in a crumpled little heap. Jeanette, who has never been called anything except Guinea because that is what Charlie named her, lay still as death.

Margaret was in the yard when the Dodge, much faster than it should have, wheeled into the yard.

"Hon," said her daddy, white-faced, carrying a limp body in his arms, "I've kilt little Guinea."

He laid her on the porch and wiped at her face with a cloth and found that she was breathing, and then she opened her eyes and Charlie just said, quietly, "Thank you, Lord."

He took her to the doctor in town, who picked the gravel out of her legs. Jeanette didn't scream, she didn't even cry that much.

Margaret, Juanita and the other sisters swear that something happened to Jeanette as she lay unconscious, because as she grew up and older she became an angel, a selfless, giving, caring woman who watches over others and lives for them.

Margaret came to call her Jeanette, Child of God, and you can argue with her about it if you want to, about what might have happened during those moments of unconsciousness, but you won't convince her otherwise.

Jeanette is noncommittal. On the one hand, it is nice to be thought of as a true saint, even a Protestant one. But on the other, it is a terrible burden. What if she slipped up, and cussed in public?

She just lets the legend roll on.

"It all depends, hon," she says now, "on who you ask."

*   *   *

There was never a quiet time for him, between his children and grandchildren, never an empty nest. Some people might have ached for a little peace, a little solitude, but that was what God made the rivers for. As he neared fifty, his life had not changed. Charlie still climbed the ladder every day with a hammer dangling from his hip, still fished when it suited him, and still seemed at his best, at his happiest, with children on the floor at his feet, or doing chin-ups on his skinny forearms. Ava loved them, too, but Charlie . . . well, Charlie just owned them, owned their hearts, as he owned the hearts of his own children. Some men are just blessed that way. Some men walk in the room, and babies laugh out loud.

# 30.

# Sam

---

To some cultures, leaving your husband is a stark, definite thing. Women of Margaret's era did not so much leave their husbands during bad times as they just went home.

"Goin' home to Momma" was the last thing they would say as the screen door slammed. It was during such a period that Sam was born.

Margaret was watching *American Bandstand* at Edna's house when the baby she was carrying let her know it was time. Her sisters took her to the hospital in Anniston—the Piedmont Hospital, the one much closer to home, had not been built—for what had become routine in their family.

But the baby was situated wrong, and it was a terrible night. When morning came, the doctor and nurses still hovered over her.

They almost didn't make it, mother and child. When Charlie came to see his grandson, he noticed the boy had scratches all over his head, from where the doctor had gripped him, trying to bring him safely into this world.

Charlie stared at the boy for a few minutes, then stuck his head in her room. "You got Edner and Juaniter beat," he said, " 'cause you had a boy."

It was that night, or maybe the next, that Margaret stood over her son in the house just off the Piedmont Highway and told him, over and over and over again, that he belonged to her, to her alone.

His daddy might have some claim, but she knew even then she could not count on him. So she just stood over him and later lay beside him, to whisper those words to him. And as tired as she was from the hard birth, she was still awake the next morning, looking at him.

"He didn't have a hair on his head," she said, and he was long and thin, but she thought he was beautiful. Juanita said he was ugly, but she might have been kidding.

\* \* \*

More and more, after coming back from Korea, Charles kept his own company. He had always been a drinker, but now he was drinking alone. And no one knew how long he would be gone, where he was or what he was doing. He showed up a little while after Sam was born. Charlie forgave him once or twice, but one day he saw more fear than anger in his daughter's face after she'd spent time with him, and that ate his guts out. So one day, when Charles Bragg came for his wife and son, Charlie just held the boy in his arms and let his daughter choose. And the dark-haired boy, no flowers in his arms this time, drove away alone.

## 31.

# Saved

---

*Whites Gap*

1957

On Sundays, he would haul Ava and the girls to Tredegar Congregational Holiness Church, a small wooden chapel where the floor would shake from The Spirit and sensible shoes, and he would sleep in his 1946 Dodge while the people inside sang and shouted and celebrated in the high holy.

He never went inside, not once.

He could have faked it. He could have slid into one of those hard pews and nodded his head as the preacher sweated, pointed and rocked back and forth on his feet, in the grip of joy. But he hated hypocrites, hated people who quoted scripture as they picked your pocket.

So he just lived by his own morality, which a lot of people say they do, but it doesn't count much if your heart is black as coal dust. The good people of the foothills could call Charlie a sinner in the purest sense, because of the likker and more, and because he never talked to God. But knowing what I know, I wonder. How many people would want to stand naked before God side by side with him if heaven was winner-take-all.

It was fall, the night it happened, one of those nights when Sam filled his boots with coal just after Charlie closed his eyes.

Margaret and Sam were living with Charlie and Ava and the younger girls in a house not far from where James and his family lived. Charlie, who said he often felt cold, had started sleeping on a sofa in the living room. He had gotten more gaunt in the past few months, but he was so bony anyway, no one thought much about it.

Margaret and Sam were asleep when she heard the door open, and it scared her. In all her life, nothing good had come from being awakened in the middle of the night. But it was just her daddy, standing at the foot of the bed.

"I remember he put both his hands on the bedstead—I can still see his hands on the bedstead even today, and he said, 'Wake up, Margaret, I want to tell you something.' It really scared me, because he was so serious, and looking straight at me, and he just said: 'I'm saved. The Lord has saved me.' "

It terrified her, because in a world of people who walked around talking about God, he had stood alone, unasking.

"He said, 'I went to bed, but I couldn't sleep. I kept hearing this music, but I couldn't tell where it was coming from. So I walked outside, and I saw that the music was coming from above, from where I guess heaven is. And then I heard a voice tell me that this was my last chance. I just wanted to tell you, tell you I was saved.' Then he walked out of the room and walked down to James's house, and told James.

"I wanted to ask him about the song," Margaret said, "but I was too scared at the time."

*　*　*

He didn't tote a Bible around, after that, or go into the church, or preach to anyone else. He just knew he was saved, just knew the voice in the sky was real. He knew he had to give up his sins, and he did.

He stopped drinking.

He didn't taper off, he just stopped.

It had to be God.

His daughters said it just had to be.

* * *

You hear stories like it a lot down here. People get saved in the tomato patch. They get saved driving to get a pack of Winstons, or get saved watching wrestling. Some people might laugh at it, but then they probably never heard music from the stars, and a voice in the sky. Wouldn't that be wonderful, though. Wouldn't that be fine.

# 32.

# The gremlin goes home

*The Coosa*

1957

They were fishing, Charlie and Hootie, not far from Hootie's old shack. They had some fried bologna sandwiches with hot mustard and a big wedge of sharp cheddar cheese, waiting in a sack stuck in the crook of a tree limb, if they got hungry. They hauled in mud cat, and Charlie talked and Hootie listened, the way it had always been. Charlie had raised much of his family in the years since he first met Hootie, and as the Bundrum children grew up and married, Hootie had grown gray and wrinkled, though it was still hard to tell exactly how old he was. He didn't help Charlie on the rooftops anymore because he was creaky and stove-up on the cold, wet mornings, but he still bundled up his clothes and climbed on the old car or truck when the Bundrums moved, still found an empty corner to lay his belongings and make his bed, still sat on the porch and rolled smoke, but now it was the grandchildren he handed the empty tobacco pouches to when he was done.

Though he was much older than Charlie—that much was plain—their relationship was reversed. Charlie was the father, and always had been. That was just the way it was, though from a distance, it must have looked so different, what with Charlie yammering on and on about something, and Hootie just nodding, sagely, every now and then.

When he did talk, he spoke to Charlie about being homesick for the river, but Charlie didn't think much about it. Hootie had become a permanent thing, or at least that was how it seemed.

On this particular day, they caught all the fish they could tote. When it was time to leave, Hootie said, quietly but firmly:

"I believe I'll stay."

Charlie told him not to play folly, and come on. They'd have a fish fry.

"I believe I'll stay," Hootie said again.

"But why, son?" Charlie said, but he knew why, knew it better than most people.

This dark place just had a music only a special few people could hear.

"I'll be back, by and by, to check on you," Charlie said as the little man disappeared in the gloom, in the direction of his old shack.

*　*　*

When he pulled up in the yard, Jo and Sue asked him where Hootie was.

"He went home," Charlie said.

He shouldn't have missed him all that much, maybe. Jo and Sue were still in the house, lovely, blond-haired girls who did not fight like the older children had, but who held hands and did everything together, as if from some bedtime story. They were both quiet, and they took books into the woods to read. They doted on him, too, like the others did.

But it was a long, long time before he stopped glancing over to the corner where Hootie had lain, covered up to his hat with a quilt, only his long, hooked nose sticking out, like a smokestack.

It just didn't seem right, somehow, not to holler over in the mornings, "Git up, boy, let's ketch 'em 'fore somebody else does," or pack an extra lunch for him when he went off to work.

It just didn't seem right.

# 33.

# Water without end

*Jacksonville, Alabama, and Clearwater, Florida*

MARCH 1958

Y ou can swing a hammer for a hundred years, swing it all your life, and all it does is throw sparks and drive nails and get hot from the friction, but it don't bend and it don't melt and it don't even change. The handle, that part, will crack and shatter, but you either buy a new one at the mercantile, whittle a new one or get some black electrician's tape and bind the old one tight enough to last, and just keep pounding. Because the business end, the driving steel, was made to outlast muscle and bone, even will. It just plain wears a man out and then passes from his hand to his son's, then commences on him.

Even Charlie couldn't wear out a hammer.

He landed a good-paying job in Clearwater, on the west coast of Florida, early in 1958. It was the farthest he had ever been from home, but he went down and pounded nails and came home with a wad of money in his pockets. He never liked banks. How could a man ever have more money than he could carry in his Liberties? It was beyond him.

He would have stayed longer, he said, maybe even saved up enough to make a down payment on a little house, but he had been feeling puny again.

That's what he called it. Puny. Like it was a weakness, to get sick.

But he did get sick, and then sicker. He had not had a drink in months, but the doctor at the new hospital in Piedmont told him that he had lost too much of his liver, told him he was going to suffer, and he was going to die. The doctor didn't know when exactly, just that it was certain, the hurting and the dying.

Charlie walked out of there and went to work, and just kept working, for months, because pity don't feed the bulldog. But in the spring, the misery knocked his will out of him, and the hammer slipped from his big hand. It wasn't his good hammer. He had forgotten his good hammer, left it with some men down in Clearwater, along with some other tools, when he got sick down there and had to come home.

It bothered him, not having it. All he had ever been, really, was a blue-collar man. He had made some whiskey, yes, and caught some catfish and jack salmon, but he was a roofer, mostly, a man who worked with tools—with that hammer and a level and a handsaw— and he didn't really have much to leave, except them.

"We got to go get them tools," he said to Ava, and Ava told him to hush, Charlie, stop worryin' about them damn tools.

They had moved back to the Cove Road, not the same house, but close. The grandchildren still came and he still doted on Sam, but a gloom was on him.

In March, William and Juanita helped him into the backseat of William's like-new 1956 Chevrolet. It was two-tone, blue and white, and as pretty a car as has ever been made.

They headed south, to get his tools. They had made a bed in the backseat, and he lay there, propped on pillows, wrapped in a quilt, as they glided between the pines.

He slept hard and long. He was still asleep as his children

crossed into Randolph County and into the little town of Wedowee, where a police cruiser pulled in behind them, and the officer turned on his flashing light.

\* \* \*

Juanita was at the wheel. Juanita can drive anything that rolls.

But this time she had a little trouble with the gears, and the tires squealed a little as she found second, and that is enough in Wedowee to get you arrested, on a slow day.

They had a white plastic jug full of water between them on the bench seat, and as the officer strolled up he pointed to it.

"Is that likker?" he said.

William, who even as a grown man still had a little of the devil in him, picked the jug up and shook it so hard that little bubbles formed on the rim at the water level, the same way he had seen Charlie shake that moonshine in his beading bottle a long time ago.

"Got a fine bead on it, it sure does," he said, and laughed, and then the officer took the jug, unscrewed the cap and sniffed it.

His face fell.

He told the Bundrums to try and be more careful, and walked stiff-backed to his cruiser. Charlie, apparently asleep in the backseat, had not even opened his eyes.

It was his last brush with the law, the last time they tried to hang a likker charge on him, and he slept through the whole damn thing.

\* \* \*

It was a different Florida, then. The asphalt sliced through the scrub and palms and the thick oaks, so different, so alien, from the up-country forests. It had a loneliness to it, a loneliness that Floridians dream about today. The hottest thing going was the gator farms, and you could see a man wrestle one if you wanted to. The orange groves stretched as far as you could see, in places, and the smell of the rotting fruit reached out to them.

It was cold, for Florida, and they rode with the windows rolled up tight. Charlie got cold easy, then.

He got bored in the back. He told William to pull over and let him drive, and even as a grown man, William found it hard to say no to him.

He had never been behind the wheel of a car as fine as this, a car William bought with his steel-plant money. He had never been behind the wheel of a car that could go as fast as this.

William and Juanita dropped off to sleep, but William soon awoke to the sound of the asphalt rushing, loud and fast, beneath the car. No matter how tight a car is, it has a sound to it when you turn it loose, when you pour the coal to it.

It sounds like water rushing fast through a big pipe, and that's how it sounded then.

"Old man," he said, "you pushing it a little hard, ain't you?"

Charlie did not even turn around.

"Hush, boy. I know what I'm doing."

And William closed his eyes again, and the power poles flashed past like fence posts, and Charlie looped his big hands over the wheel, and enjoyed the sound.

\* \* \*

They stopped in a grove of grapefruit trees—people did that, then— and Charlie picked a big one off a tree and broke it open in his hands, and ate the whole thing leaning against the car.

They found his tools, then drove over to the Gulf before heading home. Juanita had never seen anything like it, but the wind was cold and the sand was cold, and Charlie just stayed in the car.

He had never loved the Gulf, anyway, the way some men do. It was like Guntersville. It was water without an end to it, too wide for a footlog. Water like that, so deep blue, could just swallow up a man, and it would be like he had never been.

\* \* \*

They drove home with his tools on the floorboard at his feet, and not long after that he went into the hospital in Piedmont. It was a fine, fine hospital, people said. It was long and narrow, like a chicken house, and made from red brick. It had green tiled floors and smelled like most of them do, of disinfectant and Salisbury steak and fear. He came out on an Easter Sunday. Margaret remembers, because she took him an Easter lily.

Everyone was glad about that. They had him, again, among them. But Margaret knew something was wrong, because his eyes were shining from the wet in them.

All her life, she would hate hospitals. So many educated people, so much medicine, so many machines.

All those healers with such nice, clean hands.

## 34.

# All by and by

*Jacksonville*

SPRING 1958

Ava and Charlie had been together for more than three decades. Thousands of nights, she helped him find his bed when he came home befuddled, grinning and stumbling and singing about love and trains. Thousands more, she worried herself old waiting for the rumble of his truck in the driveway.

She dragged that cotton sack, to help pay their way, and pricked her fingers on those sewing needles, being careful not to bleed onto the cloth. But more than anything, she gave him the children that gave him a reason to laugh, and a reason to live.

Now she looked at him and wept, for him, for her, for all the people who believed that he hung the moon. And for once, it was not just Ava bawling again, but something that drove everybody else from that room, leaving them truly alone for the first time in . . . hell, could they even remember? She had a right to cry. For everyone else, he had been a wall that protected them. For her, he was the wall she threw herself against, over and over and over again.

He decided he would not die here, in this house, under her watch. He would not die here with his three youngest daughters, Margaret, Jo and Sue, watching.

Jo was seventeen, Sue was fourteen, and Margaret, though already grown, had depended on him more than anyone. It would hurt them, sadden them. But Ava, so brittle, might shatter, might never come back from it at all.

He asked Edna, the oldest daughter, the tough and sensible one, to take him home with her. She said she would put a little soft bed in the living room where the television was, and they could all watch the boxing matches and Cisco and Pancho, and Lucy.

"I'll cook special for you, Daddy," she promised him, but that was not why he went with her, she knew.

"Daddy knew I was tough."

\* \* \*

Now, on the morning after Easter, he waited for her to come and get him and take him away.

He fretted as the morning passed into afternoon.

"Lord," he said, within Margaret's hearing, "I wish she would come on."

Ava went and sat in a bedroom, and stared at the floor. She could not bear looking at him, the way he moved without strength, without purpose.

Sam toddled around the floor, but Charlie did not seem to notice him much. Margaret could not bear it, the sadness in the house. She moved from room to room, silently, but her mind was screaming.

Finally Charlie noticed the baby boy, who stared up at him, unblinking.

Charlie could not pick him up, he had gotten so big, so he just reached down and touched the top of his head.

"You don't let nothin' happen to him," he said, looking at his daughter. Margaret nodded. He had said it before, so many times, but then it had been a command.

Now, it sounded like he was begging.

"You can't let nothin' happen to him."

He paced feebly around the house, and every few minutes he would look out the front door and mumble: "Come on, come on."

Later, they heard Edna's car coming up the drive. She had gone to get the bed, and it had taken her longer than she thought.

"Thank God," he said as she drew closer.

For as long as Margaret could remember, her daddy had worn a hat or a cap, but he walked out to the yard bareheaded. As he slid into the car, Margaret, with Sam on her hip, rushed into the house and got his cap, and ran back out and slipped it on his head.

The baby was waving.

"Bye, son," Charlie said.

"Bye, Paw-paw," Sam said.

Edna took Charlie away.

* * *

Edna cooked him some boiled okra and stewed potatoes, and at dusk he took a walk with Charlie Sanders and Mr. Hugh. It was windy, and cool. He said he wanted to walk in the cool wind.

Edna had not wanted him to go, but he shushed her. "I believe it'll do me good, that wind."

It was a fine walk. The trees and shrubs and crawling vines were in flower or already green, covering the gray bark that always looked so dead and hopeless in winter, and new grass covered a cow pasture not far from the house. Later, the night train would rumble across the Tredegar trestle, shaking the trees, stabbing the darkness with a lance of yellow light, but now there was just the dying sunlight, and the wind, rushing.

The men were passing a pasture gate when he just stopped, to get a breath. He looked around him, as if it was the first time he had seen anything like it, anything so fine, and fell onto the new grass.

\* \* \*

People came, a flood of them, to the house on the Cove Road that evening, but Ava did not greet them. She just sat on the edge of the bed, still staring at the floor, as she would do for weeks, for months. There was barely room to turn around in the small living room. Women filled up the house, and men thronged the yard, smoking, talking. For Margaret, it was like a dream.

People hugged her and told her what a fine man her daddy was, but even with so many people encircling her, with so many arms wrapped around her, all she could think was, "Lord, I ain't got nobody."

Later in the evening there was yet one more knock on the door, and she looked through the screen door to see her husband, Charles, on their stoop. He was wearing his black suit.

"I'm sorry, Margaret," he said.

\* \* \*

The cars lined the blacktop for more than a mile the day of the funeral.

Tredegar Congregational Holiness Church couldn't hold the people. They filled the pews and stood in the back and along the walls, and everyone said how it was good that it was not hot, with such a crowd. Most of them were people like him, working people, and they came in their mechanic's jumpers and overalls and shirts with a name across their breast pocket, and the heavy work boots thudded across the planks as they walked by the casket. Women wore ancient felt hats and homemade dresses, the hardness of their eyes and the tight set of their jaw just a foil for their soft hearts and gentle natures, and they cried even before the preachers made a sound. Outside, their children, safe from all but the vaguest thoughts of death, sat miserable in cars or pickups, under threat of a prolonged whipping if they made any racket at all.

Inside, mixed in with the denims and faded floral print dresses, were the dark wool and store-bought dresses of the town people and the rich landed farmers, whom Jo called the Big People. They had closed their drugstores and left their shops and offices and come to be here, for this man who dug their wells and built their big gray barns and waved at them from the rattling cut-down, who made the finest likker on either side of the state line.

Charles Bragg, who had killed at least one man with his bare hands in Korea, sat beside Margaret and cried like a child.

He did not respect many men, but he respected her daddy, her daddy's strength. When Charlie had ordered him from his door, something he might have killed another man over, he had just bowed his head and left.

Now he took his son, Sam, and walked up to the coffin, and together they looked down on Charlie's face.

The casket was plain pine, something he could have made himself. In it, the man showed no sign of the sickness and the agony that had consumed him. His hair did not have a speck of gray.

He was still, the women mourners remarked, a pretty man.

Margaret could not stand to look at his face. As she paused beside her daddy, she looked instead at his hands.

The undertaker had dressed him in a blue suit, but the hands did not belong to a man who wore suits. His hands were rough and scarred and callused, his nails thick and cracked, his knuckles and the joints in his fingers red and swollen, from the work.

A lifetime of grease and tar and river muck had worked into the skin itself, and under the nails. A working man's hands never really get clean, no matter how hard you scrub.

*　*　*

The funeral singers, women and men who traveled from death to death, offering their skills, sang about the mystery of death and the beauty of living, which was a fine idea, considering the man.

> *Farther along*
> *We'll know all about it*
> *Farther along*
> *We'll understand why*
> *Cheer up my comrade*
> *Live in the sunshine*
> *We'll understand it*
> *All by and by*

Hoyt Fair and Big Fred McCrelless, two mighty men of God, preached him home.

Big Fred could not preach for crying. Charlie, the onetime whiskey man, had been his friend. He had been one of the people Charlie loved to talk to when he saw him in town.

Fred, built like a refigerator with a hat, could boom from the pulpit and send sin scrambling like a spider for a dark hole, but now his voice was low and soft. The good of the man just overwhelmed his faults, he said.

"Ava, James, William, Edna, Juanita, Margaret, Jo, Sue," he said. "I loved him, too."

Hoyt Fair, a man with a stern, harsh face who shoved Satan aside the same way he knocked down trees with his big yellow bulldozer, was oddly humbled, and said he belonged down there with the family—his son, Ed, was Charlie's son-in-law.

The two men painted a picture of a man with courage and heart, a man who was a defender of the weak and a smiter of the wicked, a man of charity, but one who never asked for it. They praised him as a fine father, which was the gospel, unbending truth, and as a fine husband, which was true mostly and anyway it was a funeral.

They said he had found God just in time, and then everybody prayed, and the funeral singers did "Gathering Flowers for the Master's Bouquet."

> *Gathering flowers*
> *For the Master's bouquet*
> *Beautiful flowers*
> *That will never decay*
> *Gathered down here*
> *And carried away*
> *Forever to bloom in*
> *The Master's bouquet*

Grown men cried in the pews as they sang, which does not mean anything unless you know that type of man.

* * *

After that, Ava often retreated from the world to sit on the edge of her bed. Sometimes you could hear her singing a funeral song, not from Charlie's service but from her own momma's funeral, long ago.

> *In the sweet by and by*
> *We shall meet on that beautiful shore*

*In the sweet by and by*
*We shall meet on that beautiful shore*

She missed him terribly, but maybe not as much as the others did. Because she still spoke with him, from time to time.

\*   \*   \*

No one had expected Hootie to come to the funeral, and he didn't. He would have been terrified of the people, all those people, and he only could have stood it if his tall friend had been beside him.

If Charlie was, as his Bundrum cousins claimed, the last bridge between those old, wild days of the river and this more civilized time, then Hootie's path between those worlds vanished with the death of his friend.

Charlie had kept his promise to look after him, and he would even go fetch the little man and ride him around on errands. But after his death, Hootie was never seen in town again.

Not long after Charlie died, they found Hootie's homemade boat caught in a snag on the river, and not far away, they found the little man dead on the bank.

As in his life, the rumors swirled around his death. Was he beaten to death for his money, or had he dug it all up and planned to flee in his boat, but been caught? With no champion to shield him, did they come for him in the night?

Or had he just gotten old and lain down to die in the dappled shade, in a place where he could see the sun dance off the water?

In time, most people forgot he had ever been at all. But when people talk about Charlie, they will snap their fingers and a smile will creep across their face, and they will say, "Hey, remember that little ugly feller, the one who followed Charlie round like a dog?"

His name was Jessie Clines, and he was unvarnished proof that my grandfather was a good man.

* * *

For his family, there was something much worse than grief to live with.

"There was a silence, then," Jo said of her family's life, after Charlie was buried in town. Ava almost never mentioned Charlie. The children almost never mentioned him. "It was just too hurtful," said Jo, who was only seventeen when a lifetime of silent mourning began.

What a funny legacy for a beloved man, to be pushed out of the minds of the people who loved him, to have the mention of his name all but vanish from the day-to-day language of his family.

But it had to be that way, to go on living.

Ava did not go crazy. She went to work. She had cracked, but did not shatter, and she chopped and picked cotton for Walter Rollins and in Mr. Homer Couch's fields, and picked blackberries, to sell by the gallon. In a war, they would have called her one of the walking wounded.

Her hands got infected and they swelled up so big it hurt Jo to even look at them, and her legs were scratched bloody because she still believed a lady did not work in pants, but she worked on.

She was clumsy with an ax but she chopped their firewood herself, and every third whack, it seemed, a block of wood would kick off the chop block and slam into her bony shins, and she would cuss under her breath and whack at it again, and when she got mad she would flail at it so hard and fast and wild that passersby could not tell if she was chopping wood or just beating it to death. When she was done, her legs would be bloody.

Where she hurt most, no one could heal. But Ava had two daughters at home. Jo and Sue were in high school and junior high school, and clothes had to be bought and lunches paid for, and rent made.

Jo and Sue picked cotton with her, but everyone knew Jo would be gone soon. A good-looking boy named John Couch was courting her, and it was just a matter of time before he asked her. Homer was his daddy, and Jo would pick cotton in her school clothes—her nicest clothes—to try and catch his eye, and she did. "He had brown wavy hair, real wavy," said Jo, and she made Margaret and even Juanita come to that field one day to see him, and they said that, yes, he did have a head full of hair.

The older girls helped when they could. When Jo was taking typing in school, Ed and Juanita bought her a typewriter on credit. "They went into debt for me," said Jo.

To escape the sadness of the house, Sue tagged along when Jo and John went to the fair or to town or to the drive-in. She was perhaps the most beautiful of that family. She was a cheerleader at Roy Webb Junior High School, and a queen at the Halloween Carnival. She made good grades without trying.

Her life, outside that place of mourning, was a happy life, but she never understood why her daddy had to leave them so completely. The death, she understood. But she wondered why her daddy could not come and visit, in stories and memories, the way others did. Only Ava, in the middle of the night, said his name aloud. He came to visit her, and just her, but that was only because of the cracks in Ava's mind that let him slip through.

\* \* \*

Margaret came and went, often, from that sad place. She had gone back to her husband after her daddy's death, because Charles Bragg had been kind and decent at the funeral and because there was really no place else for her to go. But the whiskey twisted him, so she drifted from one house where she dreaded the sound of a car in the driveway to the now cold place where her daddy was everywhere, and nowhere at all.

# 35.

# Backbone

Margaret was grown now, and three children pulled at her skirts. Three years after she had Sam, she had me, and three years later, Mark. And three years after that, she had a baby who died soon after birth.

For twelve years, her husband had shown her flashes of warmth and kindness, but he fought his war, still, and drank his paycheck, and he let his babies do without.

And now and then, a taunt from Margaret's childhood would echo in her mind.

"Scaredy-cat, scaredy-cat," the other children had chanted, because she was meek and seldom fought back. But it hardly mattered then. She did not need any backbone when her daddy was alive.

Now she hated herself, for just absorbing it, for taking it, for not showing the strength her daddy would have shown, to . . . to what?

The last thing her daddy said to her, had begged of her, was to protect her children, and she had done that, every day for twelve years. She stepped in front of her husband's rage, meekly, her eyes cast down, shielding her children. How much more backbone that must have taken, to do that, than to strike him down, as her daddy would have done.

And now, on a winter day in a raggedy white house in the little community of Spring Garden, on the day when she saw that his demons had him for good, she found the backbone to walk away.

She got up from the kitchen table and started putting her babies' clothes and toys into brown paper sacks, and they walked away down a railroad track, walked away for good.

She went back to Ava's house, and she let it be known that she was taking in ironing for pocket change a pound. When fall came she asked Mr. Walter Rollins if he needed cotton pickers, and he did.

Sue had married a boy named Jimmy Sweat and moved out, so it was just Margaret and Ava and the three boys in the house, unless you believe in ghosts.

And if you do, can you doubt that when he spoke to Ava, when she sat up in her bed with her silver-black hair streaming down her back, he told her he was proud.

# 36.

# Ava

*The foothills of the Appalachians*

In the mountains north of Rome, on a cold April evening in 1932, Ava left a baby girl. Four decades later, sitting in the backseat of a silver 1971 Chevelle, she went back to find her.

Juanita wheeled the car along the narrow black ribbons of asphalt, past tumble-down barns that had the command SEE ROCK CITY painted on the roofs in letters big as a Frigidaire, past red-brick churches with marquee signs that warned HIS TIME HAS COME AGAIN, past junkyards where green waves of kudzu had covered acres of rusted, picked-over cars. The hills got higher as they rolled northeast, through cotton and timber land and textile towns, past the bait shops, Dairy Queens and plywood signs that offered "pecans to pick, for halves." The Chevelle's six-cylinder motor did not rumble, it hummed. The vinyl still smelled new.

Ava was sixty-five, a widow of fourteen years, and was living at the time in a Jim Walter Home beside Juanita and her husband, Ed, on the Roy Webb Road in northeast Alabama. If the pulpwood trucks stayed out of their way, Nita would have them in the Georgia foothills in two hours or so. Ava, her long hair bound in a silk scarf, turban-like, for traveling, was quiet, but she was always quiet when she traveled, as if the motion itself made her sad. Juanita cannot recall the day precisely, but it was too late for a big coat and too early for dogwoods, so it must have been March.

In one hour they had crossed the Georgia line near Cedartown and were easing into Rome. There, they got a Double Cola for Jeff, Juanita's fussing three-year-old, and picked up Ruby Crider, a second cousin on my momma's side who had lived her life in west Georgia, and knew the roads.

Ruby, who would talk a courthouse statue to dust if it ever made eye contact, gabbed nonstop, blue-streak, bullhorn-loud-and-opinionated for the next few miles, as was her prerogative, stopping her oratory just long enough to emit a quick "Turn here" every few minutes. They drove up Highway 27 to Turkey Mountain and went left just before the River Bridge, ending up in a wide place in the road. "Curryville," Ruby announced, as if she had led them to Solomon's mines.

To make sure, since there were no signs, they stopped at a house there and asked an old man in overalls if they were where they wanted to be. The house had gourds strung on lines around the well house and yard, and they bumped and rattled in the breeze as the white-haired gentleman, the retired postmaster, peered into the Chevrolet's backseat.

Ava rolled down her window, to be polite.

"Miz Bundrum," he said, like they had last seen each other only yesterday, not forty years ago.

"How do," Ava said.

"How is your husband?" he asked.

"He has passed," she said.

"I am sorry," he said.

He gave them a gourd—gourds make fine birdhouses—and told them how to find West Union Baptist Church, the last leg on the journey. They found it on a hill, a small, wooden place, brilliant white, dwarfed by a large graveyard. It did not strike the travelers as unusual to see such a large cemetery around such a tiny church. Not everybody kneels, but everybody dies.

They pulled around to the back on a dirt road and got out. If there was any noise, any noise at all, Juanita cannot recall it. Even Ruby, who had talked without drawing a breath on the world history of gourds, was quiet now. Ava looked around her at the maze of graves.

"I remember a holly tree," she said.

Then she started to walk fast, in a straight line, as if she came here every day, and stopped at a nondescript pile of stones. She began to cry.

"I watched him," she told Juanita, "so I'd know."

Emma Mae, eleven months old when she died of dysentery in April of 1932, was her fourth baby, coming after James, William and Edna, and before Juanita, Margaret, Jo and Sue, and the only one she had left behind.

The pattern of rocks that Charlie had laid on her grave so they could find her again was still there, moved about by time a little bit, but still there.

It should not have taken forty years, maybe, to stand over the grave of her daughter, but her life, which was her husband's life, had tugged her quickly away from here. This quiet place, the last time she had seen it, had been one more scene in a rearview mirror for a family who roamed the hills and valleys like gypsies, searching for a living, preoccupied with hard, bitter times. Still, after all those years, all those journeys, she remembered.

When they left for home, not much later, Ava twisted around in the seat and stared out the back glass, until the pretty little church and the neat cemetery vanished around a curve, taking with it the only piece of real estate that she and her husband had ever owned.

* * *

Ava lived twenty-two years after that. When she was in her seventies she lost another daughter, the lovely, sweet-tempered Sue, to cancer, and my aunts were so protective of her brittle mind they did not tell her for a long time. In her last years her mind and character, so tightly strung all her life that the devil could not help but use it now and then for a trampoline, frayed and weakened so much that she became sweet and demure as a child. Her violent outbursts and cussing jags faded, and her silver eyes clouded, and her skin became white and thin and translucent. There was, it seemed, no place in her anymore for her mischief to hide.

She lived her last days in my aunt Jo's house, in a room crowded with dolls and stuffed animals. But every now and then she would wink at me, as if to say, "Yes, I've got 'em all fooled," and she would whip her harmonica out of her dress and blow up another hurricane.

Her daughters doted on her, but there was a difference in the love they had for her and the love they had for him. They had, over a long lifetime, had to care for her as much as she cared for them, and perhaps even more. She could not have survived without them.

He had burned brighter, and had not asked anything from them. He was gone much too quickly for that, leaving images in their minds of his will and strength and power, of kindness and gentleness, and joy. His flaws vanished. She only got old.

Then she was just gone, on a November day in 1994.

And an odd thing happened.

Her children stopped talking about her very much, because it hurt them so bad to touch her in their memories, and what good is that?

## 37.

# Always in summer

---

*The foothills of the Appalachians*

PRESENT DAY

The foothills vanish altogether in the winter, when the rain and the low clouds drift in, turning everything steel gray. Then the temperature drops and the rain freezes solid to the pines, and the weight of it snaps off their limbs with a sound like pistol shots, and you can stand and listen to it, like a pitched battle in those woods, if you have the time.

But now that I have a picture of my grandfather, one so much finer than torn black-and-white, I imagine him always in summer, always in his boat made from two car hoods welded together, feeling for the mud and sand of the bottom with the end of his pole. The boat glides and glides.

I try, sometimes, to picture myself there with him, but as a boy of six or so again, not as a man. Because I don't know what he would think of me, grown.

But a boy, now.

A boy.

I bet he would give me some candy, and sing me a song.

*Apple pies grow on bushes above*
*And the crust is flaky and light*
*Roast pigeons fly into your mouth*
*And the sky is always bright*
*There's a lake with stew and dumplings, too*
*Cakes to be had for the askin'*
*And time seems to fly 'neath a sugar sky*
*As you spend your whole life baskin'*

—A SONG FROM THE GREAT DEPRESSION

# Ghosts

***Jacksonville, Alabama***

John Henry died young, working himself to death as he beat a machine in a race for his own self-worth on some mythical railroad track. Big John died saving miners trapped in a cave-in. Crockett died in the Alamo, killing Mexicans. All myths and legends, made precious by stories of sacrifice and shortened lives.

Charlie was no myth, and not even a legend, really. Or at least, just a small one.

It is only when you compare him with today, with this new South, that he seems larger than life.

The difference between then and now is his complete lack of shame. He was not ashamed of his clothes, his speech, his life. He not only thrived, he gloried in it.

Maybe it's harder now. More complicated. A friend in Alabama told me the story of some ol' boys working at a chicken plant: about how, while they were on a cigarette break, a single bedraggled chicken escaped through a half-open door and into the courtyard where the men were squatting in the gravel, blood and guts specking their clothes.

An assembly-line worker from inside chased the chicken round and round the courtyard, but the men on their break just smoked and watched. Finally the chicken got up just enough speed and got just enough wind under its wings to cheat fate and the ground, and it soared over a chain-link fence to freedom.

And, after a moment of disbelief, all the men in the courtyard began to clap.

"You know," one man said to another, "that chicken did something you and me ain't never gonna do."

The realities of this new, true South are not as romantic as in Charlie's time, as bleak and painful as that time was for people of his class.

The new, true South is, for people like him, a South of mills that will never reopen, of fields that will never be planted again, of train tracks that are being turned into bicycle trails.

In the new, true South, it is harder to be poor and proud, harder to work your way into an unapologetic, hard-eyed independence. I think Charlie could have done it still, but he was more man than most. Imperfect, sure, but a man. A kind mostly lost to this world forever.

You see ghosts of them from time to time. They live in good men like my uncles and my brother Sam.

Now and then, the ghosts come back and spank us a little, as a reminder. I recall a time not too many years back when I walked into Brother's Bar in Jacksonville, Alabama, and saw my grandma's brother, Fred Hamilton, sitting on a bar stool.

The only job he ever had was picking guitar. He never married. He just picked his guitar and saw the country.

I'd thought he was dead. But there he was, in a pair of brown and tan two-tone shoes and a checked sport coat.

"What you doin' here, Uncle Fred?" I asked him.

"I'm sitting here and drinking this beer," he said, "and then I'm gonna go over there to that pool table and take some money off the college boys."

And he did. He was eighty.

I watched him, wishing that he was someone else, and then I walked out into the summer night.

A lot of people, I know, never knew their grandfathers. But I will hate this, hate it until the day I die.

But even from the grave, he affected my life.

From the grave, he affected everything.

\* \* \*

Even before I got to the reunion, I knew how it would be. On the plane I shut my eyes and imagined, blocking out the screaming babies and yammering tourists who were coming home from the theme parks and had the gigantic rubber rodent ears to prove it. A voice on the intercom said we were "circling over Alabama," but I was already there, disappearing into it just as completely as if I had pulled one of my aunts' quilts up over my head.

Under two-hundred-year-old pines at Germania Springs, weathered gray picnic tables would creak under gallons of potato salad, endless deviled eggs and barbecued everything. The fried chicken, cooked in iron skillets by old people or just purchased at the deli by the young, would send a smell of salt and grease and crisped flour into the breeze as men in neatly pressed jeans trimmed their nails with razor-sharp, Tree Brand pocketknives and eyed the coconut cake with bad intent. Sam and the Roper brothers would talk puppies, football, cotton mills and lures, but not politics, because no matter who is in office, it will change nothing about life down here.

The women would sit in the lawn chairs and talk about work and babies, even if those babies were now six foot two, and their children, big and small, would ask them a hundred times, "We eatin' yet, Momma?" My aunt Jo would chase after a great-niece named Ava, threatening the toddler with wet kisses and an Instamatic. She would catch her and old women would gather around and say that the little girl, named for my grandmother, was the prettiest thing that they had ever seen.

The soft Southern accents, not quite a drawl, not quite a twang, just natural, would mix with the sound of ice rattling into plastic cups and a drone of distant trucks on Highway 21, until somebody in authority would beckon us to the tables with a simple "Well, it's ready. Y'all come on." Some people would pray first and a few would just close their eyes, and I would eat until I was miserable and moan about it till someone produced a cold chicken leg and a glass of tea as an antidote. I would take it, because no matter how full you are, one more chicken leg will not hurt you if it has already been prayed over.

And I would be glad to be there, to see old people I might never see again, to see cousins I played hide-and-seek with in a dark yard specked yellow with lightning bugs, back before we were scared of life and snakes.

Then the plane touched down at Atlanta's Hartsfield International and the picture in my mind vanished in a grunting herd of traveling businessmen running hard for their too-tight connections and rental car counters, cellular phones jammed up to their ears, every single one of them dragging a little-bitty rolling suitcase behind them. I always marvel at that—a two-hundred-pound man pulling a ten-pound suitcase.

What would Charlie have thought of all this? I think he would have laughed out loud, and stopped off at the bar on Concourse B.

I got in there among the herd—I carried my bag—and was swept all the way to Hertz, where I politely asked for a Ford.

It was a pretty day, and once I escaped Atlanta, it was pure country all the way home. As I drove to pick up my momma and take her to the reunion, I passed the Bonds family enclave and noticed that Gary Bonds's mailbox was still too close to the road. Every day, it was a tiny miracle if someone did not hit it with their sideview mirror or just run it down altogether if they met a car coming on the narrow two-lane road. It was not just that the box sat so close to the blacktop but that it was on the surprise side of a sharp curve, so at night it seemed to jump out at you, like a deer.

That might have made some people back their mailbox up a little bit, but not here. Gary, who went to school with me at Williams Junior High School and helped me push my Camaro when the battery was dead, once played a basketball game with a wrist so swollen he could barely stand to hold the ball. But when Coach Steve Green asked him if he wanted to sit down and heal, Gary just said no sir, he reckoned he'd just play. Like most of these ol' boys here, he will not quit and he will not change. He owns the land right up to where that blacktop begins, and if he wants to put his mailbox in the path of destruction, he will.

Some people would call it an act of defiance. I believe Gary just likes his mailbox where it is, and it always makes me happy when I manage to evade it. We would all be disappointed, I believe, if we drove by and saw it planted safely back in the right-of-way, as opposed to occasionally being knocked there. Gary should have been a Bundrum.

My momma was standing in the door when I drove up. She says she can hear the car slow down on the road, but I still don't know how she knows it is me in it.

"You miss Gary's mailbox?" she said as I stepped out of the car.

"Oh yeah," I said.

That got us to talking about mailboxes in general. My little brother, Mark, said he had planted his mailbox well off the road, but while it had never been hit by a passing car, it had been shot several times. The mailbox shooting came at about the same time that someone broke into his house and stole his guns, which was too much for him to stand.

"I don't even have to open my damn mailbox to read my damn mail," he said from behind a wreath of smoke that, even from across the room, I recognized as Camel nonfilters. "I can read my damn mail standing out in the middle of the damn road, it's got so many damn holes in it."

I said that was a shame.

"I wouldn't be so damn mad," he said, "if I didn't know they was shootin' my own damn mailbox with my own damn guns."

I nodded my head.

"Well," he said, "they can just kiss my ass and call me Shorty."

I nodded again.

I decided to ask him later exactly what that meant.

When it was time to head over to the reunion, I asked my momma, in defiance of my rent-a-car contract, if she wanted to drive. She said no, the car looked too new. I offered to drive it through a mud puddle first, but she said she was afraid to, because while she had driven for much of her life and once owned a 1956 Buick, she never had a driver's license. Things like licenses, for hunting, fishing or driving, did not impress us very much. If you live far enough back in the country, it is not crucial, even in the year 1999, to always have proper paperwork.

We pulled up to the springs at dinnertime, which is nowhere near dark down here. I parked on a chert road and we just sat for a minute to let the white dust blow away. Under the shade, old women were popping the tops on Tupperware and laying out food, and it was like I had painted it in my mind and hung it from the trees.

Germania Springs was still clear as a wineglass and so cold it burned, and crawfish still backpedaled across the smooth brown rocks and took shelter in the tender watercress, which my momma used to pull and cook in bacon grease. Cajuns would have laughed at us for eating a weed and ignoring the crawfish, but back then I didn't eat anything that looked that much like a water bug, unless there was money on it.

There had been a killing here when I was seventeen, but we tried not to think about that. The better memories wrapped themselves around it, over and over, until you barely remembered it at all. We used to know the very tree it happened under, but I looked for it and couldn't find it.

It seemed like every Bundrum in creation was in the shade of the pines, which is not grand shade but better than no shade at all. There were only a hundred or so people, truthfully, but the reunion was the first time in a long, long time I had seen all the close relatives and distant cousins in one place. Old women hugged my neck and said they were glad to see me, and it made those air kisses of Manhattan seem like, well, air.

There was a jet pilot from Texas and some middle-class retirees from Plant City, Florida, but most of the people here were blue-collar, people who pull wrenches, spin yarn in the maddening clatter of the mills, make steel-belted radials at Goodyear in Gadsden, climb poles for Alabama Power, scald chickens for Tyson, drive dump trucks, saw pulpwood, answer phones in the police department, raise hogs, preach, farm, cut hair, raise children and, when life gets a little sideways, work off their fines. My brother Sam was there, talking about the mill. He cuts the steel bands off bales of cotton using a set of bolt cutters. The bands split with hundreds of pounds of pressure and the steel sings through the air, sharp and deadly. But the pay is better than a man can make for a safe, easy job, so he shields his eyes with goggles, armors his arms and torso with leather and goes to work, trusting in God and luck, and the medical plan.

I guess what I am trying to say is, these are people who earn what they have, people with Charlie Bundrum's blood in them. Even if it weren't for the ears, you could tell by looking at them, at their big hands, the sandy hair, the fact that they can listen to and engage in two conversations at once. If that isn't proof these are his kin, I don't know what is.

They did not have to come far to be here, most of them. They live within fifteen minutes of each other. They say with great pride that they only have to stop at one intersection to visit each other, that their children ride the same school bus route that they used to ride. The bus is new but it is often the same number, even the same bus driver. I can't recall the bus number that came by our house, but I remember it was a Mr. Ted Parris who drove it, and that I went to sleep on it one day when I was seven and Sam, out of meanness, got off and let it carry me almost to Piedmont. My momma didn't whip him, but she should have.

For most of them, there was no reason to ever leave. Even in the failed economic promise of the so-called New South, in a land of boarded-up mills and overgrown farms, this is home and home is not something you remember, it is something you see every day and every moment. Sam, Mark, Momma, her three surviving sisters and one brother—the other moved off to Birmingham—live within only five minutes of each other, and have since Charlie Bundrum died.

They had been movers, true, but that was only because of Charlie. They had no choice but to follow him, and now they have no choice but to stay. Where he died, they live. They will not quit on the place where he lays.

Now my aunts think a trip to Anniston, fifteen minutes away, is a damn safari. Rootless as children, they will find the most amazing reasons not to travel, saying their dogs will run off or maybe even starve, though it is a stone-cold fact no dog ever starved in an hour and a half.

What a reason to become part of a place—that grave. Yet we are part of it, even those of us who left, came back, left again and are even now trying to make it back one more time, maybe one last time.

We became familiar faces at the Food Outlet and the Winn-Dixie, and Young's store and Snook's, McFall's and E. L. Green's and Wright's and Tillison's, buying sweet snuff, unfiltered cigarettes and Little Debbie snack cakes every payday, and pork chops every Fourth of July, buying a dollar's worth of gas when it was a dollar and a half a gallon. The old men behind the counter learned which of us to extend a little credit to between paychecks and when to hang up the CLOSED sign when we thundered up in a jacked-up, pastel blue 1969 Mustang with five-hundred-dollar Cragar mag wheels and two-dollar used tires bought from a man named Houston Jenkins, a sun-faded, blue-and-gold tassel from high school graduation dangling from the rearview mirror, and Tony Joe White blaring from one speaker—only one.

For good and bad, it was our place. It was not unheard of to see one of us accepting an award on one page of the newspaper, flip the page, and see another one of us being led off in handcuffs. We played ball for the Roy Webb Hawks and the Williams Panthers and the Ed Fair Landscaping Dirtdaubers, and joined but did not excel in the 4-H club, except for my girl cousin Charlotte, who has always been a teacher's pet.

Our mommas got the GED and jobs at Fort McClellan, and we filled space and sometimes even learned something in the red-brick schools. We got Saved here, we backslid here—and everybody knew about it—and some of us just got mightily confused. Our cars' motors swayed on chains from the limbs of trees, and our pickles and jellies and leftover baby clothes sold at yard sales that were really just bait to lure people into the yard for gossip, or just an excuse to sit awhile with a sister you were officially mad at and missed something terrible. Why else would you sit all day for a net profit of a dollar and seventy-two cents?

We got to know people, but mainly, we got to know each other. We know whose potato salad has green onions in it, and whose don't. We know who grows the best tomatoes, and what time to go visit, so as to be sure to get some. We know not to call Aunt Nita at one o'clock when her story is on, 'cause Juanita does not answer her phone As the World Turns.

Our mailboxes have rusted in the ground.

* * *

About two o'clock, the descendants of the Huguenots lined up for banana puddin' and scraped the Tupperware. I didn't even know Huguenots liked banana puddin', but I guess everybody does. As for me, I never did find out if the food was as good as I had made it seem in my mind. Word was out I was looking for stories about my grandpa and it took all afternoon to hear them, until the last comatose baby had been carried off on her daddy's shoulder, until the last pieces of cherry pie had been wrapped in aluminum foil. I scribbled notes and nodded my head and didn't eat a damn thing.

By sunset, decades—centuries, really—had slipped by beneath that adequate shade. We took a hundred pictures, but Juanita's do not count because she always cuts off the top of your head even when she tries really hard not to. I think, now, she does it on purpose.

Everybody told everybody else how good their food was, which they would have done even if it had been terrible, and my cousin Charlotte, Edna's baby girl, told me I could come live in her basement in Atlanta if I ever lost my job.

"My dog smells bad," she said, in warning.

I told her if it ever came to that, I would not be particular.

My uncle Ed told me he had retired, but I know that means he will now only work about half a day on Saturday. Uncle John's mother, Mag, had been sick, so he did not come to the reunion. Everyone told my aunt Jo to tell him "hey," to tell him that they were praying for her.

In the dusk, I walked with Momma to the car carrying an empty gallon jar.

"They must have liked your tea," I said.

"It wasn't sweet enough," she said.

It would have put somebody with high blood sugar into a coma.

I noticed as we got in the car that the chert road had streaks of red dirt in it. When I was little, I would always find a patch of it when it rained, just to feel the clay squish between my toes. Ask anybody from Alabama or Georgia to tell you what that feels like, and all they will do is smile. You can't tell about it with words, with just words.

All this, all this sense of place, of family, of love, from the fact that a dead man, a man I never even met, lies in this ground. If he had died across the river, I would have been a Georgian. If he had died in the Arctic, I would have been an Eskimo.

* * *

Sometime later, I went prowling through my momma's basement. In the corner of a downstairs bathroom, an ignoble spot for a family heirloom, I found what I was searching for—an old kerosene lamp.

It was made of heavy glass, thick as a Coke bottle, and it was yellowed and smut-streaked, but it had a few inches of fuel in its bowl and a new wick.

"Is that it?" I asked my momma.

She nodded her head.

I had grown up in the same house as that lamp, the one Ava used to cradle in her arms—instead of one of her babies—when Charlie loaded their lives on that truck and moved, and moved and moved. But I didn't know its story then. The lamp was just another knickknack in a room so crowded with them it looked like a flea market, lost between the plastic flowers and ceramic Santa Clauses and three dozen pocketbooks.

It made sense that she would have given it to my momma. Of all her girls, Margaret needed a warm circle of light.

Momma told me that it had been in her other little house the day it burned back in 1993, and that—even though it had been full of kerosene—it had somehow survived. It should have exploded into a million pieces, she said, but it didn't. The glass was too thick.

"They don't make them that good no more," she said, and I said I guess not.

I asked her why she kept it downstairs in a bathroom no one ever sees, and she looked at me like I was simple in the head.

"Well, honey," she said, "that's where I need it. That's where I go when there's storms, when the power goes out."

I had bought my momma three powerful flashlights, to use when the power goes out. I got those indestructible, rubber-coated kind, the kind that won't break if you drop them. I didn't want her to use a lantern because it could start a fire if she dropped it.

But of course, that would never happen.

And, I guess, a ghost would walk right on past a flashlight. There's no magic in a D-cell.

"Well, I guess it's made its last trip, at least," I told her, being all philosophical. But she told me no. Someone will need it, a generation or two from now. Someone always will.

It seems, people here say, that the weather is worse than it used to be, like the storms come harder and more frequent, knocking down power lines. People blame the fact that so many trees have been hacked down, or the hole in the ozone layer, or, like Ava, they blame the men who walked on the moon.

Or maybe, it is only because there is no one left to clear the sky.

ACKNOWLEDGMENTS

*I want to thank Edward Bundrum for his research on the family history and Lori Soloman for her help with historical research, and especially I want to thank all the people, kin or not, who re-created Charlie Bundrum for me from their memories. I also want to thank Jordan Pavlin, my editor, who set oil upon the stormy waters. And Amanda Urban, who knows how to roil 'em up.*